WHEN THE SECOND MAN
WAS A
Woman

Tales of twenty-one RCMP detachment wives
from the 1940's to the 1970's
and including historical background
of many detachment locations

Compiled and Written by Ruth Lee-Knight

Edited by Heather A. Punshon, Ph.D.

Illustrated by Frank Wilson

The opinions expressed in this book
are not necessarily those of the author

Published by IMAGINE PUBLISHING

IMAGINE

When The Second Man Was A Woman
Copyright © 2004 by Ruth Lee-Knight
All rights reserved.

Front cover: Ruth and Jack Lee-Knight
by Michael's Studio, Humboldt, Sask.

National Library of Canada Cataloguing in Publication Data

Lee-Knight, Ruth, 1934-
When the second man was a woman : tales of twenty-one RCMP detachment wives
from the 1940's to the 1970's and including historical background of many detachment
locations / compiled and written by Ruth Lee-Knight ;
edited by Heather A. Punshon ; illustrated by Frank Wilson.

Includes index.
ISBN 0-9736410-0-2

1. Police spouses—Saskatchewan—Biography.   2. Royal Canadian Mounted Police—Biography.
3. Saskatchewan—History—1945-   I. Punshon, Heather Anne, 1941-   II. Title.
FC3216.3.A1L43 2004   363.2'092'27124
C2004-906077-5

Layout and Design by
Lapel Marketing & Associates Inc.

Printed by
Houghton Boston Printers · Lithographers

Editor
Heather Punshon, Ph.D.
Saskatoon, Saskatchewan

Published by
Imagine Publishing
104 - 420 Heritage Crescent
Saskatoon, Saskatchewan
S7H 5P3

IMAGINE

DEDICATION

This book is dedicated to RCMP Detachment wives
especially those whose stories are told here,
and to the many wives who passed on
without having an opportunity
to share their Detachment experiences.

Table of Contents

FOREWORD

R uth Lee-Knight has given us, through this book, a first hand look at a unique part of history in the West. We believe one of the least known facts about the Royal Canadian Mounted Police was the part played by wives on small detachments in the early years of the Force before 1980. Each wife was, in effect, the Second Man. For those who served in that capacity, this book will bring back many memories. What an excellent job Ruth has done of documenting these stories. It is an accurate, informative account of the responsibilities and effort the wives were, more or less, expected to shoulder in making detachment operations successful.

Detachment husbands did indeed work long hours with rarely a day off. We remember one year when we were set to go on leave, Tom was determined we were not going to miss a minute, so we took off at 12:01 a.m. on the day our leave started. On his first day back to work, the patrol sergeant called at 7:00 a.m. to make an insignificant inquiry. It was obvious the real reason was to make sure Tom was on duty.

Ruth writes vividly about her life during her husband's years in the Force with its ups and downs. And then, in the latter part of the book, she tells us about the many situations that arose in the lives of twenty other detachment wives. We do not believe their efforts were acknowledged nor was full credit ever given by the "powers that be".

An interesting aside to the stories is the research Ruth has done on the history and present day status of many detachments mentioned in the book.

Ruth is to be congratulated on her foresight in chronicling these stories that preserve "pioneer history". The result is a most enjoyable "read" for everyone.

Doreen and Tom Light

Editor's note:

Tom and Doreen Light spent all thirty-five years of service with the Royal Canadian Mounted Police in "F" Division (Saskatchewan) and "D" Division (Manitoba). Tom was commissioned in 1966. He had reached the position of Chief Superintendent before retiring in 1983.

ACKNOWLEDGEMENTS

I want to thank all the willing participant wives who took time to provide me with their stories. Their experiences are representative of most other detachment wives.

My thanks go out to Penhandlers, a Saskatoon critique group, which I am proud to be associated with, and whose members provided much support and encouragement throughout the writing process.

I am most appreciative of the Saskatoon Library System and individual librarians who provided willing assistance. The History Room yielded information on many of the communities mentioned in this book.

My gratitude goes out to several individuals who encouraged me or helped in various ways during work on this manuscript: Isobelle McFadyen, Enid Kunkel, Dr. Heather Punshon, Lois Simmie, Tom and Doreen Light, and Assis/Comm. Bev Busson.

Unfailing technical assistance was provided by my husband, Jack Lee-Knight, who kept the printer supplied with paper and ink, and who kept the computer gremlins at bay. I am ever grateful for his help during this book's development, and for his patience when meals and laundry were often delayed, and I was further impressed when he stepped in to aid in those areas.

INTRODUCTION

While recording my detachment experiences as the wife of an RCMP member, I wondered about my mother's experiences. My father had been a member of the Force before I was born. Decades later, when I became most interested in my parents' RCMP stories, my aged mother's memory had become unreliable, and she has subsequently passed away, as had my father before. My elder sister, Marjorie died in 1995, and my other sister, Dorothy, was too young to remember anything of the years our father was in the Force.

These factors evoked in me a stronger desire to preserve my experiences and those of other wives who served with their husbands on small detachments. I was convinced there were many anecdotes worth sharing, but I was also concerned they were in danger of being lost to history (more properly, herstory).

It became my mission to seek out "herstories" and to record them in a suitable manner. I began the search for names and current addresses of prospective contributors. I started none too soon, as I discovered many detachment wives of the 1930's and 1940's had poor memories, were too ill to participate, or had already died. This knowledge only served to motivate me to accelerate my research.

The lives led by RCMP Detachment wives in the mid 20th century were unique. We formed a sort of second Force then, each of us being a back up for the man-in-charge. Our experiences will not be repeated by others since times have changed, as has the structure of the Force.

The RCMP motto is Maintiens le Droit or Maintain the Law and is inscribed on every uniform shirt we wives ironed smoothly hundreds of times throughout our service. While our husbands maintained the law, we detachment wives did the best we could in the situations in which we found ourselves.

The era chronicled here is from the 1940's to the 1970's with earlier, pertinent historical background included. RCMP history has been well and frequently recorded in book form, television and the big screen. Even so, few Canadians know anything about detachment wives. We often led strange lives, battling loneliness and fear, and many other exceptional challenges. Humour, often seen as such long after the fact, surfaced throughout our detachment days.

Readers interested in Canadian history, those who value strong marriage partnerships, and who celebrate strides made by women in society, will be gratified. What follows then, is about the partners, in every sense, of the famous men in scarlet at RCMP Detachments.

1

A Helping Hand

The RCMP constable suddenly swung open a cell door. He had just discovered the prisoner had hung herself with her pantyhose. As I happened to enter the Kamsack cellblock at that moment, he yelled to me, "Get some scissors, quick." I turned and bolted passed my visiting mother who had been touring the new office with me. I raced into our residence through the adjoining door. Grabbing my sewing scissors from a kitchen drawer, I was back in the cellblock in seconds. I again passed my mother who had turned toward our residence wondering what had gotten into me. The constable was holding the dusky prisoner up to keep her from strangling. I cut off the offending hose. The young policeman eased the coughing woman onto the bunk. We heard her draw in a first breath, and her respirations became rapid and stertorous. I found her pulse to be quick and bounding. In the next few minutes her colour and vital signs returned to normal. The constable looked markedly relieved, and more so shortly after when the matron arrived to begin her shift of guard duty.

Returning to our residence, I found my mother waiting at the door and looking quite puzzled. When I explained why the tour was postponed, we decided a cup of tea would be in order.

The above incident, which took place in the late 1960's, is only one of scores I have recorded from the 1940's to the 1970's. I doggedly preserved my detachment experiences and became determined to seek out and record others. The result is an embroidery work of this small but poignantly important design in the pattern of our country.

2

On Marrying the Force

It was probably predestined that I marry a Royal Canadian Mounted Police member, and a tall one at that. I never thought in those terms, however, until some time after Jack and I were married. In my childhood home at Humboldt, there had always been a photo displayed of my father in full red serge uniform. The family album held other less formal pictures of him with his fellow policemen. Daddy's engagement in the RCMP was short-lived, for him more of an adventure than a career, and it had all taken place before I was born. Photos and stories of a time before my memory held a fascination for me.

I often poured over old pictures trying to imagine what life was like in the time they represented. How could this tall, handsome, apparently carefree, young man be my dad? The photos showed little resemblance to my older, care-worn parent. What was the name of my dad's mount, and that of the dog that trailed behind? Although many of my questions went unanswered, there was always one fact my sisters and I had impressed upon us. The Royal Canadian Mounted Police was an honourable, highly regarded institution, and members were to be given unquestionable respect.

While my sisters and I grew up in the difficult 30's and 40's, our home was like many others, where, for several years, the head of the household was away serving in one of the armed forces. Daddy, who had been in business between his stint with the RCMP and the outbreak of the Second World War in 1939, sold everything, putting us into a maintenance-free apartment before joining the Royal Canadian Air Force. With his background experience, he was signed up as a military policeman. He looked handsome in his new uniform, although not as attractive as in his scarlet. More photos of him and fellow airmen adorned our walls, and another album joined the first.

When on leave, Daddy would often bring home two or three other servicemen, usually young and far from their own homes. My impressionable child's mind easily and unconsciously absorbed the idea that a man in uniform was not only attractive and respected, but also greatly desirable. Indeed, my older sister, Marjorie, went to dances with airmen, and after the war, married a former member of the R.C.A.F. This was my background when I went out into the world.

3

RCMP Recruits and Student Nurses

In 1956 I was to go to nursing school. Many girls from Humboldt went to Saskatoon, the closest city. I, on the other hand, decided on Regina because my sister, Marjorie, lived there. As it happened, this decision helped strengthen my regard for men in the Force. With the RCMP Training Academy located in Regina, it was quite usual, I found, for student nurses to become acquainted with young recruits while skating at the Stadium or when attending a dance at the Trianon Ballroom. Young nurses and recruits were further encouraged in their friendships by dances held at the nurses' residence. Our school supervisors extended a formal invitation to the recruits via their instructional supervisors. It appeared both institutions of learning held a mutual belief that the two groups of young people exerted positive influences over one another. It was in the best interest of each school to encourage affiliations with socially acceptable, well-regarded members of the opposite sex. What better combination, some highly placed minds must have thought.

It was true that young nurses and recruits had a number of characteristics in common: most were dedicated, thoughtful, caring people preparing for careers in service to others. It could only improve each image to encourage fraternization with the other. (It didn't escape my attention a few years after my marriage and since, just how many members of the RCMP had married registered nurses).

It wasn't as though students of our nursing school, Regina General Hospital, dated recruits exclusively. There might have been one girl in every class or two who would date a medical intern doing his in-service at our teaching hospital. But most interns, having previously attended university in other cities, were often already married, or engaged. Those not spoken for were often too short, balding, covered in warts, or otherwise quite unattractive.

There were other students at home from the University of Saskatchewan. There were also Regina's divinity students, bankers, accountants, provincial government employees, and farmers, and at least one professional hockey player, besides RCMP recruits, all crossing the threshold of the nurses' residence.

They would present their well-groomed selves at the entrance desk, presided over by a crisply starched, dour-looking residence supervisor. Each young man would give the name of the student nurse expecting him before sitting quietly and uncomfortably in the large foyer with its vaulted ceiling, tall, polished windows, and immaculate, marble floors. When the nurse-date appeared at the desk she would sign the register showing her absence from residence. On returning, she would sign again before the designated deadline. Descending the stairs to the foyer, she and her nervous date greeted one another in a subdued manner, both anxious to be away from the gaze of the evening supervisor. Outside the heavy, oak doors and down another set of broad steps, the dating couple would follow the curved sidewalk until they disappeared.

There were always a few student nurses who tried to remain true to hometown sweet hearts, but long separations almost always resulted in broken relationships. Fortunate were the couples where both the girl and her beaux were from Regina, and could continue dating as before. My hometown sweetheart didn't approve of me dating others or even dancing with anyone else when out with him. Perhaps we weren't right for one another in any case. My destiny was as yet awaiting me. I went on to date some very nice chaps, some from the RCMP Academy and others. I was not, however, ready for a serious relationship at that time in my life. I had my studies to concentrate on, and then I planned to move with three classmates to work in British Columbia. We were going to travel.

4

One Thing Led to Another

Fate stepped in. My father's illness resulted in postponement of my plans (permanently as it turned out) and I moved home to Humboldt. I soon was on staff at St. Elizabeth's Hospital. Within the first year following graduation and passing my Registered Nurse qualifying exams, I met Jack Lee-Knight, a tall, curly-haired constable with the RCMP who had recently been transferred to Humboldt. Before long we were *going steady*.

My parents seemed to approve of Jack. Predictably they were pleased that he was a member of the RCMP, and it was important to them that he was a church-going Protestant. In 1956, Roman Catholic and Protestant parents were still intensely wary of mixed marriages. For all my growing-up years I had been made aware of the gulf dividing people of different faiths. I silently grieved the pain that it had caused many in our community. It didn't seem right keeping apart those who loved one another. I'm happy the situation has improved considerably over the years. But back in the '50's, the stigma of marrying outside one's church was a consideration of paramount importance. This would not pose a problem for my parents with Jack as a prospective son-in-law.

They were further approving to discover he was an active member of the Masonic Order as was my father. With all the positives Jack represented, they raised no objections to him being from a race other than British; Dutch was all right with them. The way was clear for us to continue dating and to our eventual engagement.

One day I showed Jack photos of my growing-up years. My sister, Marjorie, had given me the album some years earlier. Jack pointed to the golden embossed figures of two cherubic children in traditional Dutch clothing on the album's cover.

"And this would be our future family, no doubt?" Jack asked, grinning.

"I'm sure it is," I said and we both laughed. As it happened, when our own son and daughter were small they actually did resemble the drawing. Later, I marvelled at the coincidence of owning an album with likenesses of small Dutch children on its cover.

Bridal party on steps of Humboldt Post Office, 1958

5

Welcomed into the Fold

Early in our relationship, I learned of RCMP esprit de corps. A member's fiancée or wife was given special consideration. She was watched over and protected by other members when her man was on duty. Sometimes a second, single member accompanied us to the movies or when we'd go out for a cup of coffee. Jack's fellow officer and closest friend, George, would accompany me on a date when police work kept my fiancé on unexpected, extended duty. Sometimes Jack would join us later, but if not, George would see me safely home.

I enjoyed the special attention, but at the time I didn't recognize this first indication that I'd be *marrying the Force* when Jack and I took our wedding vows. That realization became clearer in the first years of our marriage, but before that, my attention was taken up in choosing furniture, planning my wardrobe, going to showers given in my honour, and in wedding plans.

We were married at St. Andrew's Anglican Church in the summer of 1958. The small white church had served our family since I was a baby. My sisters and I had attended church and Sunday school there, and had been members of the choir. Our confirmations, my sisters' weddings, and their children's baptisms had all taken place at St. Andrew's. The church was polished and smelled sweetly of flowers from my mother's garden. While a dainty bouquet was attached to each pew, tall vases held bunches of colourful gladiolus and peonies. Every pew was filled with relatives and friends on that sunny, pleasant Saturday, August 16, 1958.

Again, members stationed in Humboldt rallied around. d'Arcy Morrice, a senior member in the Force, and a lay reader in our church, assisted our minister in the communion portion of the service. Two of the fellows, Ed Corson and Dave Wilson acted as ushers and drivers. George Wootton, of course, was a best man along with Jim Riley whom Jack had befriended at a previous posting. The sergeant-in-charge of the detachment had just been transferred to Humboldt so he graciously offered to man the office while all other members took part in our wedding. All the fellows looked resplendent in their dress uniform of red serge tunics, highly polished Wellington boots and in banana pants, so-called by the members because of their snug fit and yellow side-stripe.

My bridesmaids were Lilly Wittrock, one of my best friends from nursing school, along with my sister Dorothy Utigard. They wore aqua chiffon gowns. My niece, Connie Dickson, my sister Marjorie's four-year-old, was a sweet flower girl dressed in aqua. Donna Woodham, a high school girlfriend was the soloist. I loved my frothy white gown featuring a hoop skirt in keeping with the day's fashion. Seed pearl embroidery and French lace inserts were tastefully incorporated into the design. My lacy garter was "something blue". Sonja Myrheim, a dear friend from nursing school had lent me the headpiece from her wedding at which I'd been a bridesmaid. My veil flowed from the borrowed crown, there were three dozen organza-covered buttons trailing down my back, and my billowing, full skirt swept the carpet with a luxurious swish. I carried a florist's creation of all-white blooms, including large roses, sweetheart roses, and stephanotis. The only touch of colour was a spray of green, English ivy.

Following the service, we were thoroughly showered with confetti on the church steps. We went to the photographers while our guests enjoyed cold refreshments in the banquet room of the Princess Café. It was finally time for Jack and I to relax with our guests for drinks before we all convened to the United Church hall for the dinner reception. Before leaving on the first leg of our honeymoon trip to Niagara Falls, Jack and I said our good-byes to our families and those friends present at my parents' home.

Our guests had painted our new yellow and white Chevrolet with pink calcimine, written messages on it and added traditional trailing tin cans. One of the physicians noted that our luggage consisted of everything but the kitchen sink so he thoughtfully provided one for our trunk. When we finally made our get-away, heading for Saskatoon, we noticed friends in two vehicles following us.

Laughing, we waved at them, thinking they'd turn off at any moment, or surely at the town's outskirts. When they continued to tail us after we'd left the town behind in a cloud of dust, we were slightly uneasy wondering about their intent. Jack turned onto the driveway of a farm and parked on the far side of the house, quickly turning off the car's lights. After two or three minutes of suspense, he put the car into gear and slowly moved around the house and back onto the highway. Our friends had also been waiting quietly in the dark, but when our car appeared, the driver called out, "It's okay, Jack, we're in no hurry. Take all the time you want. We'll stick with you."

"Oh, no," I said. "Now what are we going to do?" However, soon our practical jokers turned back and, at last, we were on our honeymoon.

6

Our First Home

Within three weeks we were settling into our first home. It was an apartment over the post office in Humboldt. The three-story brick structure on Main Street boasted a clock that chimed the hours. This residence was intended for the man-in-charge of the RCMP detachment. Since he preferred to rent a house when he transferred into town that summer, Jack and I were required to live in the apartment. The office and rooms for single men were also housed on the second floor. As a new bride, I was getting used to the positive and negative aspects of living only a few paces from the detachment office and single men's quarters. Although I didn't recognize it at the time, here was another indication of how I'd *married the Force*.

Three single members walked by our door to get to their bathroom. They didn't always remember to wear something more than a towel and this was sometimes embarrassing if we met in the hall. Still, the guys were like family and we enjoyed their company. We didn't have a phone, so if Jack's assistance was needed in the middle of the night, one of the fellows would knock on our door before walking into the apartment. Many nights I woke up to find one of them standing beside our bed explaining the latest problem. Jack could sometimes give the young constables procedural advice on the spot, but usually he got up and went to the office.

I resumed working at the hospital and when at home I made an effort to cook. My offerings left much to be desired, so I'm sure it was a great treat for Jack when we were invited to a meal at my parents' home. Whenever I think of the kitchen in our first home, I recall smoke drifting out of the oven where I was cooking pork chops. When Jack suggested the meal must be ready, I merely wafted the smoke with a tea towel.

"Mom said it takes thirty-five minutes," I persisted. We've both laughed many times over that silly scene. I also followed my mother's recipe for making buns. Jack ate the results like a good fellow, but I knew my small, firm buns were nothing like Mother's airy creations.

New detachment building at Naicam, 1959

7

First Child and First Detachment

The following summer, Jack repaired the small, wooden crib my father had made years earlier. I painted it white like the chest of drawers and an oak rocking chair, and placed matching decals on all three pieces. Soon the nursery was ready and we looked forward to becoming parents. We were thrilled with our handsome, curly-haired son born on the maternity ward where I worked. My parents were beside themselves with joy, having a grandchild living only a few blocks away. I enjoyed pushing Christopher Todd's carriage around town, showing him off to friends before going to visit his grandparents.

Humboldt, located east of Saskatoon, was established in 1905 when the Canadian National Railway built its main line through town. This community is part of St. Peter's Colony that was begun by the Benedictine Brothers, instrumental in the purchase of 100,000 acres of land. Humboldt is the base for a large farming area and its economy supports many successful businesses. It is the long-time Home of the Humboldt Flour Mills. The RCMP offices were housed on the second floor of the post office until a new detachment was built. The post office building became the town's museum. Humboldt's population is over 5,000.

Forty years after moving from Humboldt I was to revisit that detachment and suite. The exterior looked unchanged but the interior had undergone a major transformation. It was strange to find a chapel where the main office had been. A replica of a 1940 hospital room and an old style dentist's office occupied rooms that had been sleeping quarters for single members. Our old kitchen and bathroom had changed little. I was taken aback to discover the nursery, our bedroom and the living room had been made into one large area where the hardwood flooring was covered with earth for displaying stuffed wild birds and small animals common to the area. From camouflaged speakers came the sounds of appropriate bird songs.

My bubble of happiness soon burst when I first heard we were to be transferred to the small town of Naicam. My parents were upset, but we all knew the transfer was a good career move for Jack. He was to be in charge of his own one-man detachment, this at the young age of twenty-five, and he was very pleased. I was proud of the faith the Force was putting in him, and I tried to be happy for him. When Jack told me the detachment was scheduled to have a new building, complete with two-story living quarters, I felt my spirits lift. In any case, Naicam wasn't far from Humboldt. By the time the moving van came for our belongings I was as excited as Jack.

Two-month-old Todd cried all the way to our first one-man detachment. We made the forty-mile, dusty trip to Naicam along gravel highways #5 and #6 in the summer of 1959. I drove our private car, and since Jack was the better driver, I asked him to take our first born in the patrol car. Little did I realize the baby, bundled up on the passenger's seat, would wail all the way, likely protesting the bumpy ride and without benefit of being held in comforting arms. The more Todd cried, the warmer he became and the faster Jack drove. Both father and son wanted that trip over with.

When we pulled up to the Naicam Hotel where we would stay over night, I rescued my red-faced, sweaty child. With tears in my own eyes I comforted him and he soon settled, although he whimpered occasionally even in his sleep. In the years to follow, there would be many trying situations for our family when we strived to conform to the Force's demands.

8

The Old Quarters

Early the next morning, we drove a few blocks to our first one-man detachment home, a building which was nothing more than a small, old bungalow. We had seen it the previous year when visiting the couple stationed there. Now with neither furniture nor curtains, the house looked dreary and uninviting. The office, which had once been a bedroom, necessitated the public's passage through the living room to enter it. The upstairs, an attic really, with low slanting ceilings, served as a bedroom. It was a relief to know our residency there would be only a temporary arrangement as new quarters were being built. We would be the first occupants of the two-story brick combination office/cell/living quarters upon its completion in only a matter of weeks. Buoyed along by Jack's excitement and enthusiasm, I was prepared to make the best of our housing arrangements. Initially it was an adventure.

Jack immersed himself in his office, quickly familiarizing himself with its equipment, supplies and current files. Once the moving van had deposited our belongings indoors, Jack was anxious to make his presence known in the community and to study names and locations of the village's businesses. He stayed long enough to set up the crib and help locate a few other infant accoutrements. He happily agreed to my suggestion that we would simply "camp" in our present location. I thought it wise to unpack only necessities since I so trustingly believed we would be in the new place shortly. The packing boxes and five-foot wardrobes would remain in the living room; there was no other place for them. We could sit on our sofa but couldn't see the other side of the room or the window because of boxes.

A stove and refrigerator were provided for the kitchen, and later that day Jack would set up our chrome table and chair set. Once Todd was fed and settled in his crib upstairs, I quietly checked the premises, peering into cupboards and the bathroom. It was a relief to see water taps at the sink, but a disappointment not to have a flush toilet. It was unsettling to think of what the substitute might be when I crept downstairs to the musty basement.

After adjusting to the dim lighting, I saw the small area was encased by crumbling cement and held an ancient looking furnace. Behind the furnace, where there was even less light, I made out the shape of the septic toilet, which was to be the bane of my existence for long months to come. It seemed antiquated to be without completed plumbing in 1959.

Making a quick retreat upstairs, I thought of my parents' modest but comfortable and certainly more modern home. The nurses' residence in Regina where I'd lived for over three years was almost palatial, and even the apartment we'd just left in Humboldt had more conveniences than my present address. As a registered nurse with a new baby I was most concerned about proper hygiene. It's fortunate that this is only a temporary situation, I thought.

When Jack returned, he set about the task of wrestling our mattress up the narrow and winding stairs to the attic bedroom. The movers had already established that the passage would not admit the seven-foot box spring. That's all right, we decided; we'd manage fine with the mattress on the floor; after all, we were camping. The attic's stained wallpaper was peeling in several spots. Other than Todd's small crib, there was no other piece of furniture in the room; the space didn't allow for anything else. The heat was oppressive and there wasn't a window to open. After a few nights of sweltering heat and little sleep we had to make a change.

Jack squeezed the mattress back downstairs and placed it on the box spring, which almost filled the dining alcove. Once again there was room only for the small crib beside our bed. We had no drapes on the windows, but we could get more air and were able to sleep better. We changed clothes in the bathroom and hoped we wouldn't be seen getting out of bed in the morning. We thought we had the sleeping arrangement settled until 6:30 the next morning.

Jack had been in bed only a few hours when there was a loud knock on the front door. Peering out of the covers and across the living room, I was shocked to see a man looking back at me through the door's glass panel. I nudged my still-sleeping husband who quickly slithered into his breeches that he'd dropped on a packing box earlier. He yanked on his boots and went to the door as I pulled the covers over my head. This is a disgusting way to live, I thought; the new quarters can't be ready fast enough. As Jack opened the door, he was met by a farmer who said with genuine surprise, "Aren't you up yet?" Wide-awake by now, I clasped my head in disbelief. It seemed the man had brought a load of grain for the elevator, and while in town, decided to come to the detachment to check on some routine matter. It was soon apparent much of the general public didn't know there was only one man to run all the affairs of the detachment. While everyone expected the town and highways to be kept safe by the RCMP, not everyone considered that the lone man had to sleep sometime.

As a detachment wife, I was being introduced to a life of sleep disturbance and sleep deprivation. Late and early callers, or a phone ringing at any hour of the day or night, was to be a way of life for our family for many years.

The office's two-way radio squawked intermittently. Even when the house was quiet, I often experienced wakeful nights worrying about Jack. He was alone on highway patrols, at stakeouts or when doing investigative work. It was always a relief at two or three in the morning to hear the patrol car pull up, even when Jack worked for another hour or two typing out charges or other forms. Sometimes, that would be the first opportunity he had to complete subdivision reports that he wanted to go out in the morning mail.

His life, and by extension his family's, was ruled by many things, including the ever present "Diary Dates". Subdivision headquarters expected to receive each report on the date designated and there was little room for adjustment. Once a member opened a new file and reported it to subdivision, he was required to include the date on which he expected to make a further report. Even if there was no new development, the member was expected to submit a report by the designated date. When an investigation proved difficult to advance, or when the member was swamped with other work, he might request an extended diary date. It seemed to be something shameful and to be avoided at all costs.

It was amazing how well my husband could function without sleep or how he could grab a power sleep and be refreshed. He usually asked me to waken him promptly after only ten or twenty minutes. I was always relieved to see him stretch out in his lounge chair and to note his slow and even respirations. It didn't seem right to call him when he hadn't slept in twenty-four hours or more. But there was always court to get to, a witness to interview, that report to finish, phone calls to make, and other office work.

So this is detachment life, I thought. A home that isn't settled, a husband who is infrequently seen, a bed that provides little sleep, and a bathroom without a flush toilet.

There was often someone at the door or on the phone wanting the policeman, but it was a lonely situation for his wife. In a few weeks, a couple of neighbour ladies came to call. It was nice of them, but it was also somewhat embarrassing. We had to sit amongst the packing boxes in the drab living room with no drapes and with the bed just behind us. The callers had delayed their visit, allowing for house settling. They must have wondered what kind of people we were, to be living in such disarray after all this time. They were given a hasty explanation with forced cheerfulness about how we were "just camping" until the new quarters were ready.

Their visit left me even more anxious to move, but whenever I inquired about the building progress, which was easily once a day, Jack would tell me of the latest delay. Some building material hadn't arrived; they couldn't start this until that was done, and so on. He drove me over to view the progress every few days. Weeks of waiting turned into months, and we were both tired of living in our cramped and inconvenient quarters.

If we had unpacked, hung temporary drapes, had our belongings around us, the old quarters would have been more liveable. At the time we moved we hadn't thought it worthwhile. Each week that went by brought us closer to moving time, but each week also added to the others we'd already endured. It was difficult to be cheerful. I spent a lot of time caring for my small son and, after finishing daily household duties, I pushed his carriage around town. I often stopped at the new quarters, hoping to see some sign of progress.

As I washed clothes and ironed seven or eight uniform shirts each week, I planned furniture arrangements in my mind. I visually located and relocated every stick of furniture and decided on which shelves I'd place the dishes and glassware. I visualized where the last plant and picture would be in this brand new home. I looked forward to having friends and family drive in from Humboldt for visits. We'd get a dog, and Todd would have a new lawn to play on by next summer. Jack was getting to know a lot of people in the course of his duties so we'd soon be able to have locals in for coffee.

It was stressful when there was still no moving date by the end of summer. One cool day, upon reaching for the cutlery, I spotted a mouse scurrying to the back of the drawer. That sight became a moment frozen in my mind. *As if in slow motion, I can still see that mouse today, forty-five years later, its tail trailing forever across my cutlery.* I screamed. This frightened the baby who was propped up in his highchair, and he started to cry. Alarmed, Jack came bounding in from his office, only a few leaps away. By then I was crying with frustration, and was attempting to comfort my baby. I pointed to the drawer and choked out accusingly, "We've got mice living in here now."

"Oh, is that all," said my now relieved husband. He'd been deep in concentration when he'd heard my shriek and the baby's wailing. That wasn't the sort of comforting remark I needed right then.

"What do you mean *is that all?*" I stormed. "It's bad enough we're living in this dump, but now we've got mice contaminating all our dishes and cutlery."

Because there wasn't a madman with a gun at my head, and since I hadn't dropped the baby in boiling water, Jack was justified in thinking one small mouse was no cause for alarm. Then he remembered my great aversion to mice, and he took into consideration that I'd been under a lot of pressure for some time.

"Don't worry, we'll get a mousetrap and take care of that little critter," he said. He put an arm around my shoulders and tried to soothe me. "In fact, I'll go downtown and pick one up right now." All I could think of was washing everything from the cupboards and drawers in hot soapy water and rinsing with boiling water before we could eat the meal I'd been preparing.

Daily, Jack attended the trap as I didn't want to see the mice. One day he assured me there were no more mice in the house, but he kept the trap set just in case.

September dragged into October, and it seemed we were no closer to getting moved than the day we had arrived in Naicam. Still, I was determined to carry on as best I could. Laundering the baby's dirty diapers properly was quite an undertaking. I set them aside while I emptied and rinsed the diaper pail in the outhouse. Before putting the diapers back in the pail, I replenished it with water. From there, I placed the diapers in the wringer washing machine for a long chugging, and after two rinses, I hung them on the clothesline.

One cold October day, I was outside starting the first steps of the daily procedure. Stool was firmly stuck to the diaper, so I found a stick beside the hedge. Another memory was frozen in my mind that day. *I was crouched down scrapping stubborn stool off the diaper, and trying to deposit those scrapings into the diaper pail. The stool then held fast to the stick so I banged it on the pail's edge. Bits of the formed stool flew up and landed on my hands and sleeves of my jacket.* This isn't fair, I thought. All I want is one flush toilet. I finished the chore as best I could while making a mental note to give the baby a larger serving of orange juice the next morning.

Todd, new pup, Kip, and Jack Lee-Knight at Naicam, 1962

9

The New Quarters

Often in one's life, a low point is followed by pleasure, and so it was for us. Shortly after the diaper incident, Jack told me the new quarters were at long last ready for their first RCMP family. In November of 1959 we moved in.

The living quarters seemed cavernous compared to the old place. It was wonderful to unpack and discover all our treasures once more. My frustrated nesting instincts worked overtime, and the place was soon looking very homey. The building was located on a residential street at the edge of town and only one block from Main Street. There were hardwood floors throughout, with a convenient kitchen and a swinging door into the dining room. The spacious living room, a hallway, back and front entrances with closets completed the main floor. The bathroom and three bedrooms with large closets were upstairs. At last we had a measure of privacy.

There were laundry tubs and water hook-ups in the large basement. We immediately purchased an automatic washer, a clothes dryer, and a deep freeze.

It was a real pleasure for me to live in a bright, convenient home once more. I was prepared to stay in Naicam forever.

Jack was happy setting up his new office. I enjoyed having him come in for coffee breaks and meals. He'd often take his thriving son onto his lap for a few minutes at these times.

Once Todd was walking, he would sometimes wander into the office looking for his dad. If Jack were alone, he would let the little fellow stay for a few minutes. When he was about twenty months, he tottered into the adjoining office. Jack was concentrating on paper work, but he noticed Todd was playing quietly with a toy car he'd brought, and for the next couple of minutes he didn't check to see what the baby was doing. Neither did he hear him slip out the side door and into the attached garage.

We were shocked to hear the sudden, loud wailing of the police car siren. In the close confines of the garage, the siren was many times louder than otherwise. I ran from the residence just in time to see Jack disappear into the garage. He quickly turned off the siren switch, and rescued his shaken baby from the back seat of the vehicle where he had scrambled in an attempt to escape the frightening noise. Our poor child was screaming and had gone white and sweaty. As I cuddled him to me, I noticed the little white boots he'd been wearing were missing. Jack recovered them from the front seat where they'd come off when the little guy had frantically struggled to escape. All three of us learned a lesson that day.

Time passed fairly pleasantly in Naicam. We made friends, I found a good baby sitter, and worked two afternoons a week at the physician's office. Our second child, Lorie, a wished-for daughter, was born on February 15, 1962, an hour past Valentine's Day. We had been in the new quarters for two years and three months. Jack had just purchased Kip, a registered German shepherd pup. We kidded one another that I had a new baby, and he had a new baby dog. Jack planned to train the pup and be responsible for all its care and feeding.

"Don't worry about it," he said. "I'm going to keep him in the office until he's housetrained." Jack went on a scheduled night patrol the first evening I was at home from the hospital. Late that night, I peeked into the office, curious about the new pup. I couldn't believe my eyes. The office floor, which Jack kept meticulously clean and well polished, had been transformed into a doggie-do depository. There were soft, dog droppings and pup footprints everywhere, creating a barnyard odour. I remembered Jack's insistence that he would be responsible for the pup's total care. I quickly closed the door and went back upstairs to feed baby Lorie.

Naicam is located northeast of Humboldt on highways #6 and #349. It was settled by Scandinavians, but got its name from two C.P.R. contractors, Naismith and Cameron. Naicam is the centre for a fertile agricultural area, and is known for good goose and duck hunting.

In 1931 the RCMP arrived in the community. In 1958 new barracks were built on 1st Ave. N. and its first occupants were Cst. Jack Lee-Knight and Ruth with their family. The town's population is now 950.

10

Where's Onion Lake?

Just days after we'd brought our baby home from hospital, I was sitting with her in our Naicam living room. Todd was contentedly playing with toys at my feet. That's when Jack walked in with the news. We were being transferred to Onion Lake.

"Onion Lake?" I struggled with the message. "Where's Onion Lake?" He was almost as shocked as I was.

"I don't really know. Somewhere up north, apparently," he offered. "All I know is the Corporal there phoned to ask what colour we want the bedrooms painted." There had been no indication of an impending transfer, no warning at all. It was goodbye to friends, our comfortable home and to my office job. Our life was about to take a drastic turn.

There I was, on the move again. Lorie was eight weeks old, just the age Todd had been on our first move. Our family, along with Kip, our fast growing German shepherd, made the trip in our Chevy coupe. After several hours of travel and many stops to accommodate man, woman, child and dog we were all weary. Each time we got out of the vehicle we brought back in a bit more of the April mud accumulating from an early thaw. Kip was panting and twisting about in the crowded area allotted to him, and it was getting increasingly difficult to convince Todd to sit still. Everyone wanted the unpleasant journey to end.

Something was wrong. We should have arrived at our new location. North Battleford was well behind us, as was Lloydminster where we'd continued north on Highway #17 along the Saskatchewan/Alberta border. We'd crossed over the North Saskatchewan River in the vicinity of historic Fort Pitt, followed directions on a peeling sign and still we were seeing only more of the same bush country. Finally, we had to admit, we couldn't find Onion Lake. We backtracked to the tired looking sign where Jack got out to take a closer look.

The signpost was leaning at an angle, and Jack had a hunch it might have taken a bit of a twist as well. He decided to follow another trail in the bush, and sure enough, after ten minutes, we could see a white, two-story building sitting alone on a hill with the Union Jack flying above it. As we drove through the village and up the hill, the moving van came into view. I remember mixed emotions; I was glad our journey was over, but this place that was to be our home for who-knew-how-long looked lonesome and inhospitable.

Author's son, Todd, and young native woman skinning beaver
at Onion Lake, 1962

11

Looking for Friends

I tried hard to look for positive signs. I had made up my mind I would make friends with the Indians from surrounding reserves and with Métis from villages in the area. When Jack enlisted the services of a young Cree couple to stretch a confiscated beaver hide, they arrived with their little boy. I took Todd out to the garage where they were working and he was happy to see another child. I greeted his parents and tried to talk to them as they worked.

"Hello, my name is Ruth and this is Todd. What are your names?" They only giggled and held their heads down, speaking in Cree to one another and their child. "What is your little boy's name? Todd is happy to have someone to play with." They seemed to be embarrassed, and it wasn't apparent if they could not understand nor speak English well, or if they chose not to speak. "Show the little boy your trucks, Todd." Todd held out two little trucks, but the child looked down and clung to his mother's clothes. "Wouldn't you like to come into the house to see Todd's other toys?" I offered. "Come on, let's go in and perhaps we can find some cookies." The child squirmed uncomfortably as he pressed himself against his mother. I felt inept, and Todd was confused. I hadn't expected this sort of barrier, and it was a keen disappointment. These people had been hired to do a job for the "Simakanis" for which they would be paid. Their job did not include talking and they had no intention of doing so. As it turned out, their attitude was typical of many of their people in the area. The Simakanis and his family were not their people, but instead represented authority figures, to be avoided when possible. I felt especially bad for Todd who needed to have a playmate.

*Author's husband about to attend a Treaty Payment Day
at Onion Lake in 1972*

12

Mice, Snakes and Worms

It was soon discovered, we also needed a cat. Mice were found nesting in the fall-out shelter, and from there they travelled the furnace pipes throughout the house. It would seem a basement window had been left open when builders had recently moved in cinder blocks and cement in order to install the fall-out shelter.

The federal government had ordered these shelters be constructed in the basement of various RCMP buildings. The Cold War, with its threat of the Atom and Hydrogen bombs, was the basis for their reasoning. The shelter would be a place for the RCMP officer and his family to retreat to in the event of a bomb attack. After the nuclear fall-out had settled, the officer would presumably be able to carry out any orders coming from headquarters.

The building had been empty for some weeks before we arrived, giving mice a great opportunity to get established. Well acquainted with my aversion for mice, Jack dropped everything and dutifully set traps before going on an emergency cat patrol.

Blackie, a young, female cat became a part of our household. She settled in well, proving to be a good mouser, which was at least partly due to her seemingly endless pregnancies. To our children's delight, this resulted in many litters of kittens. We were always on the lookout for a good home for her many babies, so every policeman, justice of the peace, or rancher that Jack encountered was coerced into taking a cute, cuddly ball of fur.

We no sooner solved one problem than one or more took its place. I was about to make my acquaintance with garter snakes. We learned they made their way from Badger Lake, one hundred yards below the detachment and migrated to the rolling hills behind us each spring, then reversed their trip in the fall. To hear about thousands of these reptiles slithering up or down the hills was a revolting idea, but I was shocked to realize they travelled via our yard. How long did it take them to complete their migration I wondered. How long would I have to stay indoors?

Blessedly, Jack didn't tell me Kip had already killed a snake found in our back entrance. It was months later before I heard about the incident and other snake stories. The snakes were attracted to the sun's heat retained by the cement floor of our attached garage. When Jack found several on the floor, he killed some and encouraged Kip to kill others. Todd was a witness to all of this as he was playing outside when the discovery was made and so his father told him they must "keep it a secret from Mommy". There were always a few straggler snakes that never made it to the hills. One July day, I was outdoors carrying the baby while admiring the flowers I'd cultivated along the walks and drive. I caught a glimpse of a sudden movement among the plants, and when my brain registered snake I leapt and screamed at the same time. I beat a hasty retreat into the house and didn't venture out until Jack vowed he'd made a thorough negative search of the yard.

About that time, a mass of ugly, dark grey caterpillars were discovered on the north side of the building. Closer inspection revealed these creepers all over the grass and garden in the back yard. They were moving down from the bushes on the hill, across the yard and from there proceeded up and over the two-story building. It was an incredible sight. It seemed the whole animal kingdom was inexplicably drawn to our home.

Never having heard of tent caterpillars, I didn't realize there was nothing to be done about them but to wait out their mass movement. A first thought was to sweep off the offending creatures, and I started to do so with a vengeance. Working my way across the wall, I noticed the first area I'd swept was covered once more. The hose was the next idea. It's true, the water knocked off waves of worms, but they merely crept through the water and kept on their single-minded advance. I recognized defeat, so I stayed indoors for several days once more.

13

Horses and Cowboys

During the summer months, it was common to see horses hobbled on reserve land. Often during the night, one would graze its way into our yard where there was a lot of green grass, as well as my vegetable garden. The horse wore a bell that jangled each time it took an impaired step with its hobbled front limbs. Many nights, I'd be awakened by such a sound outside our bedroom window. Sometimes, I'd go to the window and rattle on the glass trying to chase my night visitor away. Other times, it didn't seem worth the risk of waking the rest of the family, so I just prayed my garden would be spared. Besides, I felt sorry for any animal intentionally disabled in this manner. The horses often overlooked my garden, being satisfied with feeding on grass.

Cows also wandered into our yard. I had to be vigilant whenever I noticed reserve cattle in the area. Because they seemed to be drawn to my garden, I wondered if their sense of smell was more acute than horses. Luckily, I always spotted the intruders before they did much damage, and they made a hasty retreat when I accompanied my hollering with the banging of pot lids.

A cattle drive passing directly outside our kitchen window was a unique experience for me. While eating our supper at the kitchen table, my children and I were witness to this unexpected event. I first became aware of approaching cattle when I heard bawling sounds getting louder and louder. I could barely believe my eyes when I looked out the window. Hundreds of cattle were looming toward us. They were surrounded by a swirl of autumn dust. The orange glow of the setting sun was a backdrop. The scene was like something straight from a western television show. Cowboys on horseback rode on either side of the fast approaching herd. I could hear whistled commands. The men waved their arms, directing the cattle.

They were getting closer to our fence. It was a spellbinding scene. Twenty feet from my view, the cattle veered and ploughed up the hills north of the detachment. As they thundered by, their pounding hooves obliterated any sounds within our residence. Blackie leapt onto the kitchen counter to look out and to mouth her complaint while Kip paced the room, panting and salivating. The children and I continued to stare at this strange moving picture. I didn't know Jack had come in from the office until he placed his arm on my shoulder.

I'd witnessed the working days of one horse earlier that summer when a well driller was engaged to drill for water on ranch property north of the detachment. At 9:00 a.m. every day the operator hitched his horse up to drive the machinery. This required the horse to plod in a circular path, stopping only when it was given a fifteen minute grazing and drinking break every few hours. I was concerned about the poor animal's treatment, and thought it should have longer breaks more often. I even felt a little guilty, as the searched-for water was to be for detachment use.

Without really wishing to see the poor, labouring animal, my gaze kept returning to the hill, as I worked around the kitchen. When the drill auger would hit a rock, the horse would hesitate while the operator went into the hole to remove the rock. If water was found, the horse could be relieved of his monotonous chore, and we wouldn't have to depend on deliveries to a basement cistern. One morning, the drilling operator went to hitch up his horse, but found it had died during the night. I felt ill. We still didn't have a new source of water, and yet the horse had died in the search.

Other horses caught Todd's attention. From the safety of our fenced yard, he admired the wild Appaloosa herd, which belonged to Happy and Edna Lifeso. Their "Diamond L" Ranch was immediately west of us, and Todd imitated sights he witnessed there. He could be seen in his little black cowboy hat and well-scuffed western boots swaggering across the yard like the ranchers, and twirling his own rope. He spoke the parts of two characters in his play world, since he was so used to playing alone. Often Kip became his horse.

When the herd was grazing further away, Todd would sometimes be allowed to walk across the pasture, past the ranch house and over to the one-room schoolhouse where Edna taught. He'd arrive at recess time when he'd join the younger children on the swings or at a game of tag. He had walked the route a few times with his father and Happy. Todd also knew the way to school from the road. Pushing the baby carriage, I'd often walked with him along the road to the school. Sometimes Edna would invite him in for twenty or thirty minutes after recess. Todd was always happy when he returned home, reporting on the story Edna had read aloud or proudly showing the paper he'd "written" on while he sat quietly in a spare desk.

One afternoon, I suggested Todd visit the school for recess. He was delighted. He waved back after he'd crawled through the fence, and had started to cross the deserted pasture. The baby was still asleep, so instead of accompanying Todd, I watched his progress from the window for most of the way. I smiled to myself. He made quite a picture, this swaggering little cowboy in his blue Siwash sweater and ever-present cowboy hat. When he was only halfway across the pasture, I was startled to see a couple of horses approaching him. I was frozen to the spot. I willed him to move quickly. In moments, several more prancing horses appeared. Frightened, I watched the small figure. He weaved his way through the legs of the herd. The horses seemed excited by the presence of this short visitor.

I was horrified, thinking about what could happen. I looked back at my sleeping baby. I tried to weigh the decision. Should I leave her and run after Todd? If I called to him or walked through the already excited animals, I might increase the risk of him being trampled. If I took the sleeping baby, I wouldn't be able to move fast enough. Her crying when she wakened, would further frighten the horses. Still, if I left her, she might wake up, fall out of the carriage and hurt herself. I prayed Todd to safety. The half-minute it took him to reach the fence and crawl through it was a long ordeal for me. I knew he didn't realize the danger he'd been in. I was still shaken when, with baby and carriage I met him on the road a few minutes later.

Todd was in for a special treat when Norman Doell, the Livestock Inspector from Lloydminster, brought out a trailer load of horses for a trail ride he was leading. With great interest, Todd watched his father help Norman unload the mounts on the road in front of the detachment. They then led out a smaller horse and motioned to Todd. Norman swung Todd into the saddle and showed him how to hold the reins while he led the pony around. I ran for the camera and captured the expression of pure joy on the face of my four-year-old.

Jack watching Todd on horse, 1963

14

Family Outing

When we lived at Onion Lake, it was rare for our family to go on an outing. If we went at all, it was usually to visit a Lloydminster doctor or drugstore, and while in the city we'd always buy groceries and a few other necessities. Jack usually brought supplies home when he had to go on police business. It was simpler than taking the children, diaper bag, formula bottles and toys in the patrol car. Jack was rarely out of uniform, was never really off duty and never took a day off in those days. So, it was the patrol car or no car.

After many weeks of not leaving the immediate area, I looked forward to one of our infrequent trips into Lloydminster. It was an occasion to dress up the youngsters and myself. I remember bathing one-year-old Lorie, getting her partly dressed and putting on her new white boots before going to her room for one of her lovely lacy dresses. Meanwhile, she had crawled back over the side of the large bathtub and into her own little tub of water. She was playing happily, new boots and all. I had to change her things and put on hurriedly polished old boots.

To get to Lloydminster in the summer, we travelled to the North Saskatchewan River and waited for the Meridian Ferry. The crossing was located near the Saskatchewan/Alberta border, thus the name. During the winter we could drive over the ice. In the spring and fall, we had to travel farther west to cross the Lea Park Bridge. This day we drove onto the ferry, which was merely a floating platform with a chain-link fence around it. It was quickly apparent there was a lot of floating debris. The trees and logs built up against the moving ferry and this extra weight redirected our course downstream instead of across the river. I wasn't sure how much danger this represented to us, but I nervously watched from the patrol car, one hand on each child. The ferry operator, with Jack's help, struggled to move the debris with long poles. This wasn't turning out to be the pleasant outing I'd looked forward to. The ten-minute crossing took over thirty minutes, although it seemed much longer to me.

Todd waving, bottom 2nd from right, visiting Onion Lake school, 1963

15

On Duty

Being alone a good deal, I filled my time as best I could. Since the children were my priority, I took them for walks, played games and read to them. When they were napping, playing together or watching children's television shows, I did my housework, baked and sewed. I read and made notations about my detachment experiences when time allowed. I also wrote long letters to our families who were afraid we would never move back to civilization, as they knew it.

I had detachment duties as well. When a female prisoner was brought into the cells, I searched her for any object or substance with which she could harm herself. A bottle of beer tucked inside bloomers with elastic in the legs, a mickey of rye whiskey between heavy breasts, a jack knife carried at the waist, elastic garters, stockings or panty hose, belts, scarves or ties were some of the articles I checked for. On a couple of occasions when a female was being transferred to jail in Prince Albert, I accompanied Jack as her matron.

That was when I called on Vicky Dumont, a gentle Métis grandmother. Pierre Harper, Jack's trusty Indian jail guard, recommended her to us. Pierre had guarded for the Onion Lake detachment for many years, and had gained the trust and respect of every policeman stationed there. I had every confidence in Pierre's judgment, and after allowing the children and Vicky some time to get acquainted, we left on our trip. After depositing our prisoner, Jack and I went to a restaurant for a meal and enjoyed some time together. The return trip also gave us a chance to talk, even though the police radio often crackled messages. I was paid for matron duty, so I used my earnings to buy small treats for the children and to pay the sitter. I enjoyed the change of routine, more so because such trips were rare.

When prisoners were in the Onion Lake cellblock, I was required to provide their meals since there was no cafe in the village. The Force paid me for this duty. I kept the fare simple and routine. Breakfast consisted of porridge, sugar and milk with coffee, while a meal at any other time of day was bacon, eggs, toast and coffee. I never got any complaints.

When Jack wasn't in the office, I was expected to answer the phone and take messages. Sometimes, it was Jack phoning to say where he was and how long he expected to be away. Occasionally, he would ask me to look up a file and give him the information he needed. At times, he'd contact me by radio. If I heard other detachments trying to contact ours, I'd go to the office and take a message. "Ten-four" was the way I learned to acknowledge a message while "over and out" completed the transmission.

As the wife at a one-man point, it would have been very difficult to avoid being involved in at least some detachment affairs. On occasion, an individual's sentence would include reporting to the nearest RCMP detachment on a weekly basis. That was fine in principle. In practice, one never knew what day or hour the offender would present himself. The member could be out when he arrived. When someone came to the door, I would record the name, time and date for office records.

Once, when Jack had to be away, he told me a certain fellow would likely report in. He mentioned this was an incest case. Oh, great, I thought as I locked all the doors after Jack left. I wondered if the man would have any compunction in taking advantage of another woman, especially if she seemed to be alone. I hoped he wouldn't show up, but I kept a wary eye on the narrow road leading up from the village and on the trail coming from the reserve.

To my dismay, I saw a heavyset man approaching the gate. He looked to be about forty years old and was powerfully built. When I heard a faint knocking on the door, I steeled myself to face the caller. I opened the inside door, but kept the screen door locked. The dark presence on the steps did not look the threat I had expected. He stood with his head bowed, and this gave me a bit of courage. "Hello," I said through the screen. "The policeman is not in just now. Would you like to leave him a message?" I spoke in my most authoritative and professional manner.

"Yes," the man murmured. "I'm supposed to report in to him." He raised his head slightly, and I immediately saw the embarrassment and shame registered there. I hadn't expected that, and I felt myself relax a little. He gave me his name.

"Thank you. I'll tell the policeman you were here," I said almost cheerily. "He should be back any minute," I lied, wanting to leave the impression that I was not going to be alone for long.

"Okay, thanks," said my caller in a dispirited voice as he turned to leave. I watched his plodding retreat down the trail, and I let out a long sigh of relief as he disappeared out of sight. I noticed my hands were damp and my cheeks felt hot. Even though I realized I had been needlessly concerned, I closed and locked the inside door once again.

The next week, another little drama unfolded. A young constable had come to help Jack over the busy summer months. The day after his arrival and an all-night patrol with Jack, they had placed a couple of male prisoners in the basement cells. Pierre Harper, the trusty Indian jail guard had been hired to monitor them while the policemen got some sleep. The baby was asleep upstairs, while Todd was playing with some dough at the kitchen table where I was making buns.

About mid-morning, the young constable was awakened by the doorbell and loud knocking on the office door. He pulled on his uniform pants and shrugged into his shirt as he stumbled out from his room at the back of the office. I heard the entire disturbance as well, and had gone to the front window to see who was at the door. I was hoping the noise wouldn't waken Jack who had not seen his bed in thirty hours.

Two native women were yelling and pounding the door, demanding to see their husbands who were in the cells. I could hear the drowsy young policeman saying, "No, you can't come in because you're drunk." The women sounded angry but they turned and left. In moments, the policeman realized his error; the Indian Act provided for the protection of intoxicated persons. He knew he was required to either place the women in custody until they were sober, or to take them to their homes. "Come back," I heard him call, but I could see they weren't paying any attention to him. His uniform shirt was open at the neck and it hung out of his trousers. It was comical to see his dishevelled hair and blurry-eyes as he picked his way across the stony earth in bare feet, all the while waving his arms and calling. But I felt sorry for the young man who was having a rough beginning at this new posting. I also wanted an end to all the noise.

"For pity sake," I muttered to myself as I watched the scene before me. I hurried to the front entrance. "Ladies, *astam*," I called using the Cree word for *come* or *come back*. "If you come back, you can see your husbands," I offered. They stopped at the sound of a female voice. "Yes, just come and sit on the steps for a minute," I said, thinking this would give the constable enough time to get his boots on and his clothes in order. The women turned obediently and came to wait on the steps. By then, Jack had arrived on the scene since all the noise was just below our bedroom.

When I hurriedly explained the situation, he poked his head into the office and said, "Let them visit for a few minutes and then give them a ride home. Afterwards, you'd better get some sleep while the guard is still on duty." I was relieved when the building settled down and the men were able to get a much-needed rest.

*Author and constable at preparations for a Rain Dance
near Onion Lake in 1972*

16

Inspection

Inspection. The very word struck terror in my heart. Our subdivision's Non-Commissioned Officer from North Battleford would be bringing the Officer Commanding that afternoon. Passing muster for the subdivision N.C.O.'s scheduled visits created a stir in the office and living quarters. No detail could be left to chance when the O.C. was coming. My mind raced ahead. I had vacuumed the living quarters and had dusted everything in sight. Mirror and window polishing came next. Perspiration was dripping from my forehead. I dabbed my face with the towel carried on my shoulder. My home was always quite clean and fairly tidy, but whenever we got word of an impending inspection, I saw everything in a different light. I glanced at my watch – time to set the buns to rise. I hurried to the kitchen.

Four-year-old Todd and eighteen-month-old Lorie were watching television. Thank goodness for *Mr. Dress Up*, I thought. Nursery songs jingled in the background. Hopefully, the children would take a nap after lunch. Jack would be starved. I'd make him a few meat and cheese sandwiches – no time for soup today. I could hear the floor polisher start up in the office. Good, he was finished scrubbing and removing black heel marks. By the time the polishing was done, I'd have the buns rising and lunch ready. Then it would be time to pull a rhubarb pie from the freezer.

"Drat," I said aloud. I had just remembered I should be pressing Jack's uniform tunic and slacks. He hadn't had time to pick up the dry cleaning in Lloydminster last week. I set up the ironing board in the kitchen, and shoved the iron's plug into an outlet. The kindergarten music was fading. The children would soon start dragging out toys I'd just put away, and I didn't have time to gather them again. I sat the children at the table with their peanut butter sandwiches and milk. They happily chattered about *Mr. Dress Up*.

As I pressed Jack's uniform, I thought about the unwritten law that the wife provide a meal and a coffee break any time senior officers came for a visit. I decided these visits were multi-purpose; while in the home, the men could unobtrusively determine if the residence supplied by the Force was being maintained properly, and if the wife of the man-in-charge could suitably meet social demands that his potentially higher rank would create. Presumably, they would notice if the "second man" had gone stark raving mad while living in semi-isolation, at which time a transfer out might be deemed necessary. I thought about the brave front most detachment wives presented. Usually, policemen had enough problems without having a complaining wife. I didn't think the inspection team would be inclined to listen to my problems.

I reminded myself that following inspection, the officer's written report would become part of Jack's permanent record. Jack was a perfectionist and I felt compelled to follow his good example. I knew he appreciated my efforts. After hanging his uniform in the hall closet, I resisted the temptation to sit with the children. There just wasn't time. Instead, I gave each a hug and a kiss. I promised myself that I'd devote my undivided attention to them for the next few days.

Two hours later, the stew was simmering and the buns were in the oven. The house was as bright as a new penny, and the children, just up from their nap, were quietly looking at picture books. Out on the driveway, Jack stood back to admire the high polish he had given the patrol car. As he drove it into the garage, I noticed the sky was becoming overcast. I hoped it wouldn't rain; mud tracks were the last thing we needed after the cleaning marathon. I'd make sure our German Shepherd, Kip, didn't get past the back entrance if it did rain.

Jack took the stairs two at a time to shower and to change from his fatigues before going to the office. I put coffee on and got out my best mugs. I was arranging cookies on a serving plate when Jack burst in from the office. He looked exasperated. I was immediately alerted.

"What's the matter?" I asked.

"Oh, the postmaster just phoned about an intoxicated female down in the village. I'll have to pick her up. Will you be able to watch her in the cells while I go for the matron? Of all times for this to happen," he said in a rush. "Our visitors just radioed in, too. Their e.t.a. is three o'clock so that's fifteen minutes from now." I couldn't believe my ears.

"Oh, great," I groaned. "I'm not even dressed." When I saw Jack's look of frustration, I added, "Yes, I'll look after everything. Go on." I turned the coffee to simmer and raced upstairs, stumbling in my haste. The children came scrambling after me.

"Read me," Lorie whimpered, holding up a Dr. Suess book.

"Not yet, Sweetie. Mommy's got to get dressed first. I'll read to you in just a little while." I felt guilty putting the children off once again. Lorie stood crying in the hallway and Todd tried to interest her in his book. "Let's sing until Mommy's finished in the bathroom," I called in desperation. "Three blind mice, three blind mice," I started, hoping the children would join in. There was only time for a quick sponge bath now. I pulled on fresh slacks and a pretty sweater, yanked the pony tail ring from my long hair, brushed it out and applied some pink lipstick. As I hurried downstairs, the children trailed after me with a few of their books. With a sigh of relief, I sank gratefully onto the sofa with one child on either side of me.

We were reading *Green Eggs and Ham* when Jack returned. I gave the children each a cookie and told them to be good while I helped Daddy in the office for a minute. I went downstairs to the cellblock below the office, and searched the prisoner for any object she could use to harm herself or others. I removed her shoes, which she could throw at anyone when she started to come to, and her pantyhose in the event she decided to hang herself. She slumped onto the cell bunk and was snoring loudly before I got to the top of the stairs. Jack secured the cell door, and quickly left to pick up the matron to guard this sleeping prisoner. After washing my hands, I returned to the children. They wanted me to read *The Three-Ringed Circus*. I left the office door open so I could hear the prisoner's snoring.

A few minutes later I heard a car drive up. With one glance out the window, I knew it was the inspection team. I smiled and hugged the children. "Well, kids," I said, "it's show time." They followed me as I rose to answer the doorbell.

Still smiling, I said, "Hello, Jack will be back in a minute. He went to pick up the matron. Would you like to join us in the kitchen? The coffee's ready." The men were soon settling themselves around the table, and they chatted with my inquisitive son and daughter. As I poured three mugs of coffee and two glasses of juice, I couldn't resist saying, "We were just having a three-ringed circus." The men looked a little puzzled. I was actually thinking of the fuss and fluster our family had been going through, but I quickly added, "A storybook, you know. Have a cookie, won't you? Do you take cream and sugar?"

Author's children with Kip at Onion Lake in 1972.
Horses on neighbour's land

17

City Lights

From our living room window, I often gazed south across a fifty-mile expanse of bush country where I could see the radio tower lights north of Lloydminster. Many summer evenings after the children were in bed, and while Jack worked in the office or when he was away on police business, I'd sit alone on the front steps looking toward those lights. I yearned to be there or any place where there were lights, sidewalks, stores, a church for us to attend, and especially children for ours to play with. And I wished for women friends.

The only woman I had contact with was Edna Lifeso, our one neighbour, and a pleasant woman about the age of my mother. Although I prized her friendship, I didn't like to drop in on her too often. She taught all day and had housework and class preparation to do in after-school hours. One evening as I sat on our front steps, I thought back to the time when we met the Lifesos just after our arrival at Onion Lake.

We had been pleased when we were invited to join them, their hired hand and visiting family members for Easter dinner. Having never been to a ranch, I hadn't realized that it was inappropriate for me to wear high heels and a good dress. I also found it had been unnecessary to dress the children in their best finery. Jack had no such problem as, in those days, he was always in uniform.

Upon arrival at my new neighbour's home, I immediately noted my faux pas since everyone but Edna wore jeans, western shirts and cowboy boots. Edna wore a plain blouse and skirt, her usual school attire, and that day she had on an apron as well. We were greeted warmly. Edna produced an old wooden highchair for Todd. "Set in," she offered.

We enjoyed a hearty country meal while getting to know the Lifeso household. I still smile whenever I think back to experiencing the reality check regarding mode of dress.

From my solitary steps, I recalled my first visit with Edna once school was out for the summer. I had walked, with children in tow, to the ranch house to see what she was doing. I had discovered, freed from teaching, Edna was then concentrating on gardening, canning berries, baking, and catching up on housework. She told me her evenings were spent mending or writing short stories.

On other visits, she bustled about her kitchen and sometimes sat with me for a cup of tea. She spoke of the area's history and about ranch life. She asked about my nursing experiences, and she was always interested in our children. Because school was out, Edna was able to spend a little time visiting, giving me the desired contact with another woman. However, with the schoolyard abandoned for the summer, Todd lost occasional playtime with other children.

Sitting on the steps, looking toward Lloydminster, I grieved once again the fact that Todd was being deprived of a normal childhood.

Not long after that evening, Jack told me that he had been chatting with Mr. Nolin, the Métis chap that delivered our water. Jack had discovered this fellow had a boy about Todd's age. The family lived some distance away, but I asked Jack to invite the child to come for some playtime. My heart lifted when their first meeting was set. I don't know who was more excited, Todd or his mom.

The two boys got on well together. Although, they didn't meet regularly, on occasions when they got together, they had lots of fun. On those days there would be two little cowboys acting out their roles.

Author's son with Kip

18

Self Preservation

I remained lonesome during the day, and more so at night when the children were asleep and when Jack was away, which was often the case. Without street lamps, the nights outside our windows were totally black. The radio tower mockingly maintained its red lights that seemed to float in a sea of darkness. I was surrounded by utter silence. I couldn't relax until I knew Jack was safely back, but often when he returned it would be very late and there would be prisoners and a guard with him, sometimes the Justice of the Peace. At such times there would be loud male voices and sometimes shrill calls from female prisoners. The typewriter would clack out charges, the phone would ring and the radio would blare its messages. Heavy boots would track across the office linoleum, and cell doors would clang. This cacophony of noise would ring through the rest of the building, but was especially loud in our bedroom, being directly above the office. While thinking of having to be up with the children in a few hours, I'd will all the noise to stop. I was too tired much of the time, sometimes reduced to weeping from exhaustion and loneliness. I was fast becoming disillusioned with detachment life. There was a growing resolve taking place in my over-taxed mind. I was convinced I had to act.

The next time the Subdivision N.C.O. came from North Battleford, I decided to make my case. It had been a particularly trying week, not improved by seeping sewer water I had to splash through when attending the washer in the basement. The chronic problem of a backed-up sewer had not responded to various corrective measures during our residency. We needed a new septic field, but until one was established, I donned rubber boots at laundry time.

When the N.C.O. came in from the office for lunch, I spoke to him about my problems. I explained I was having difficulty with the isolation, unacceptable living conditions, and lack of playmates for the children. He listened sympathetically.

"I don't make these decisions on my own," he said. "You realize, of course, I can only give my recommendations to Division, but I'll do what I can." His understanding meant so much to me. I'll never know what transpired behind the scenes, but in a few months our transfer came through.

Onion Lake is situated fifty miles north of Lloydminster as the crow flies. The first detachment wife was Mrs. John Hall. I can only imagine the difficulties that were part of every day life for her at the turn of the nineteenth century. There were nine children born to her and her husband, Sgt. John Hall of the RNWMP. They were stationed at Onion Lake from 1894 until 1910. A new Onion Lake post was built in 1895 on a site chosen by Prime Minister McKenzie Bowell when he paid a short visit to the area en route to Battleford. Temporary quarters were used until that time. The new detachment was a frame house with a lean-to kitchen and storeroom. There was a stable with twelve stalls.

During the Halls' residency at the detachment, an Indian was sentenced to one month's hard labour in 1905 for beating his wife. He had pleaded guilty to the charge. When questioned by police after his release, he said he had not beaten her. His mother-in-law had done so and he took the blame because it would have been shameful for his mother-in-law to go to jail.

After her husband's death in 1926, Mrs. Hall remained at Onion Lake for many years where she was the postmistress.

The earliest report of police activities in the area is of Cpl. Ralph Bateman Sleigh. He was stationed at Frog Lake, just west of Onion Lake, in 1884, but he and his four constables left there before the Massacre the next year.

Rev. John and Elizabeth Matheson arrived in Onion Lake in 1892 to take over the Onion Lake Anglican Mission and School. At the time, it was a flourishing hamlet with a good Hudson Bay Company store, telegraph and telephone office, successful Indian Agency with competent farm instructors, two religious Mission schools, teachers, good hospital and well attended churches. In 1898, after completing her medical training in Toronto, Elizabeth returned to Onion Lake to practice medicine.

Many changes had taken place since those days. When we were transferred there in the spring of 1962 the hamlet was no longer a flourishing community. There was no Hudson Bay Company store, telegraph office, nor hospital. The Indian Agency was at Frog Lake and the Anglican Church was in a sad state of deterioration.

19

No Crystal Ball

We were to be transferred to Goodsoil, just outside the Meadow Lake Provincial Park. There were no sidewalks, not a lot of lights, nor a church for our family to attend, but there were women and there were children, lots of them, and that fact alone was worth the move.

So great was my relief at leaving Onion Lake, that whenever asked how long we had been stationed there, I give my stock reply, "One year, three months, two weeks, one hour and fifteen seconds," I announce triumphantly.

I also maintain I could have dealt with our situation more gracefully had we been given a time frame when we were sent to Onion Lake. We had no crystal ball. Problems seemed to magnify since we had no idea how long we would remain there. An opened-ended transfer to a difficult situation left much to speculation, sometimes leading to depression.

Since those days, the Force developed policy which takes more factors into account. Transfers were soon to be accompanied by other important details for families involved, such as the number of years a particular posting would be in effect. Most often a time frame of two years would be given, information that served to provide stamina for the existing situation and hope for the future while in trying circumstances. I like to think my experience at Onion Lake and my eventual protest may have contributed in some small way to the Force's second, sober look into the realities of detachment life, especially as it exists at particular points.

Of course, I recognize that times and situations have dictated many adjustments in Force policy. The country's economics and population growth and shift, along with other factors have resulted in either the closure of very small detachments, amalgamation, or placement of more manpower at individual centres. The upshot of these factors has eliminated wives' participation in detachment affairs, and has, in fact, closed many of the smaller offices all together. The following information was gleaned during an interview I had with S/Sgt. Ken Burns, of RCMP Planning and Archives Branch in Regina, Saskatchewan.

The system of the old style detachments has evolved over the years. Instead of a one-man or two-man detachment where the man in charge did police work, report writing, and conducted many management functions, he is now free to do strictly police work. A small detachment is now called a Community Detachment and has a Host Detachment. The man in charge of a detachment is now called a Detachment Commander and there is a Host Detachment for smaller ones to report to. For instance, Saskatoon has a Host Detachment for the Community Detachments of Vonda, Colonsay, Hanley, and Delisle. When a policeman from a Community Detachment is off duty or out of the office, all calls are redirected to Regina. Depending on the situation, the call is referred to the next closest Community Detachment. This new system has resulted in freeing policemen's wives from being involved in any way with the office or police work.

These changes and others have been evolving slowly as the need arises. Dying communities are responsible for different policing approaches. In 1993 a study "Models of Policing Study Saskatchewan" was developed. When the province agrees to any proposed changes, a trial is conducted in one area. Depending on results, more areas go through alterations to suit the circumstances. District Management Teams have been developed which usually consist of one officer and two staff/sergeants.

20

Transfer to Goodsoil

Goodsoil had a population of about three hundred when we arrived there in 1963. Highway #26 that we were following north became Goodsoil's Main Street. We passed five or six businesses, the village office, recreation hall, hockey and curling arenas, hospital, school, and even some homes located on that street, or just back of it. There was one residential street to the west and St. Boniface Street forked off at the north end of Main, where it reached into the bush. The detachment was located on St. Boniface, and the Roman Catholic Church with its cemetery was at the end of the road. There were a few small homes scattered along it. The village was surrounded by farmland.

The detachment consisted of an office and the cell; a year following our transfer there, single man's quarters and a garage were built. The bungalow was separated from the office by a driveway, and was located in a setting of tall pines. A large lawn sprawled to the front of the house, and there was a vegetable garden to one side. Across the road was an overgrown field and bush with more bushes behind the property. The yard and surrounding area proved to be a great place for our children, their friends and their pets to romp.

Kip, who had always roamed free when not in the patrol car, continued to enjoy this same privilege. Blackie still regularly produced kittens; we were not concerned about mice. Blackie and the persistent wooing by a tomcat just outside a low window, provided our children with their first sex education. I answered their questions by telling them, "The boy cat puts seeds into Blackie so she can grow baby kittens in her tummy. It's something like planting seeds in the garden." They accepted the explanation readily and went about their play. Children from the village and a nearby farm regularly came to play. I was so grateful to see Todd and Lorie enjoying themselves with their new friends. I put the memories of Onion Lake out of my mind.

Before getting our home completely settled, we drove seven, tree-lined miles west to the lake. Lac des Isles was a peaceful picture that June evening. A forest of pine and birch ringed this large body of water with its islands, and a sandy beach stretched along its southern shore.

Its wild beauty impressed us. It had a small resort hidden in the woods where the road ended, and there were a few private cottages dotting the waterfront.

There was no sign of anyone around. We could hear frogs singing from a nearby pond. Contented bird-chatter from flotillas of mud hens and grebes drifted across the lake. The children ran with happy abandonment up and down the sandy beach while tossing stones into the clear lake. Shrieking seagulls dived into the water for a meal, and in the distance several pelicans lifted off the lake. Kip lapped up cool water before going off to sniff in the woods. As I gazed around my new surroundings, I took in a big breath of that pure air. There were many scents mingled together; fish, green grass, Saskatoon blossoms, poplar leaves and pine. As I drank in the beauty all about me, I could feel tension seep from my body. I knew I could easily drive out to the lake with the children whenever I wanted. After leading a rather confined existence at Onion Lake, I now enjoyed a new feeling of freedom.

The drive to the lake, along a country road, was the first of many our family made together over the next three years. Graceful whitetail doe, nibbling roadside brush, would look up at the sound of our vehicle. We watched especially closely for deer on the road.

"Deer," I'd call out when I saw one and Jack would apply the brakes while the frightened animal leaped clear of our path. "Did you see the deer, kids? They're so beautiful," I'd say every time. I never tired of watching them. In addition to enjoying the deer, trees and wild flowers, and an occasional sighting of a bear, moose or elk, I treasured our lake drive because it was a special family time. When we planned an outing, I didn't relax completely until we were beyond the village. The phone might ring at the last minute or Jack might spot someone in the village that he'd been trying to locate. Police business took precedence. The children and I remained quietly hopeful until we were on the lake road. Then we all chatted and laughed together.

Sometimes we drove north of the village and crossed the Waterhen River into which the lake emptied. The river was wide and fast flowing and there were rapids downstream. We often saw blue heron near the bridge that was only a few miles north of the village. This waterway marked the entrance into the beautiful wilds of Meadow Lake Provincial Park. We looked forward to becoming more acquainted with the area and its people.

21

Square Dancing

I was pleased when both a teenager and an older woman offered to baby sit. Jack and I joined the local square dance club where we met many people. I painstakingly made matching western shirts and dresses. To obtain our 'Jailbird badges' we agreed to have several people join us at the detachment to dance in the cell so we could qualify. When we arrived at the office, the men helped Jack pick up the mattress, complete with an intoxicated prisoner, to deposit it on the floor of the garage. The civilian guard, always hired when the policeman was busy or off duty, remained with the man. We swung up the cell's bunk and secured it to sidebars. In the confined space of the cell we formed a square of four couples and danced to the square dance caller's music and patter. The struggle to perform the dance steps properly and the bumping and squeezing that ensued were the cause of much laughter. After ten minutes of this nonsense, the caller announced we had qualified for our badges. Dropping the bunk back into position, the men picked up the mattress and returned it to the cell. The prisoner knew nothing of this event, sleeping through until the next morning.

Ralph Bighead (Wapostikwin) next to author's husband and freshly baked bannock. This was near Goodsoil in 1964

22

The Bear

An occasion for excitement occurred when Jack arrived home with the carcass of a black bear he had shot. The bear was in the pick-up truck owned by the Department of Natural Resources. Jack and his friend described their trip into the provincial park, and details leading up to the shooting. Another constable, the prison guard, Todd and I all hurried out to the driveway to see the freshly killed *cinnamon bear*. I learned that day that not all black bears are actually black. Kip was sniffing the air suspiciously and growling in low tones as the hair on the back of his neck stood up. Everyone was laughing and talking. I ran for the camera and got a couple of pictures.

Lorie, then about twenty months, heard all the activity through the open bathroom window. She got off her potty-chair where she had been concentrating and came out to see what was going on. Her chubby bare feet picked their way across the gravelled driveway. Wearing only a little white sweater, she looked adorable with her curly blond hair and bare bottom. I couldn't resist taking a quick snap shot of her. The constable, being young and single, seemed to be embarrassed with her state of undress. When I noticed his uneasy expression, I quickly scooped up my innocent child and took her indoors for some tidying and clothing.

Jack took the bear carcass to Ralph Bighead (Wapostikwin was his Cree name) who was camping on the Waterhen River. Ralph and the women with him, skinned out the animal and cut up the meat. Jack gave him all the meat except for one roast and some stew meat. We wanted to experience this wild meat. I cooked the roast with a lot of herbs as I was advised, but we didn't care for the taste. When I cooked the stew meat with beef, onions, garlic and other vegetables the dish was more palatable. We enjoyed the culinary experience, but we didn't wish to repeat it.

Jack had the hide tanned and I backed it with a piece of red felt I cut to shape. The cinnamon and red went well together. We used it as a carpet on Todd's bedroom floor. I painted the drawers of his brown chest red and made bedspread and drapes from brown and red fabric. Todd was quite proud of his new carpet and the changes in his room.

Too late, we realized we should have mounted the bear hide on the wall. It became worn and tattered-looking with time, because Kip liked to sleep there. Also Todd and his friends played on it with toy trucks, and even shot hockey pucks off it. Both Jack and I had a vague belief that we would acquire more bear hides while in the area. As it turned out, Jack never hunted bear again.

The first time we passed through the park, Jack pointed out just where he'd first seen the bear and how he'd shot it. The next time we drove by the spot, he again related the story. We were all proud of him, but I couldn't resist teasing him at that time.

Over the ensuing years, we have driven that same road a hundred times, and often one of us will grin and say, "Did I ever tell you how I shot that bear?" Forty years later we still chuckle at that.

23

Sick Bay

Our first winter in Goodsoil started out on a high note. Jack curled and was even able to play in a couple of bonspiels. I took Todd to the rink where he learned to skate while Lorie enjoyed running and sliding over the ice in her boots. At home, Todd played "hockey" in the basement. Both children used the basement fallout shelter as a play area on cold winter days. (The shelter doubled as a pantry for extra groceries.)

Although we were glad to know there was a physician and small hospital in the village, we hoped we would not require such services. The hospital building was old, draughty, and looked rather dilapidated. It had been constructed originally as a store and later was used as a school. The beds were old air base cots. I had wanted to resume nursing on a part-time basis, but there were no openings on staff. In the spring, I travelled to Loon Lake thirty miles south to work an occasional day.

A low point occurred during the first winter of our three-year stay in Goodsoil. I developed pneumonia and was hospitalized in Meadow Lake. Jack had to locate the housekeeper recommended to us but whom we had not met. She was a young farm girl who was very used to preparing meals and looking after the house and younger siblings. I came to realize we were lucky to have had her but, at the time, I felt dreadful leaving my children to a perfect stranger. I was very relieved to return home two weeks later; being with my family also accelerated my recovery.

We were usually pretty healthy, but once when Jack had a cold, he developed an elevated temperature. He kept on working, and I was quite worried about him going out in frigid weather. Days went by before he finally agreed to see the doctor. He was put on antibiotics, but went right back to work. As the medication started to take effect, he became so drowsy that he had a hard time thinking clearly, and he knew he should not be driving. He was forced to lie down, although he wouldn't take his uniform off; Heaven forbid! He slept like a baby all afternoon and again that night. The next day he started to feel better and I was greatly relieved.

24

Rubber Boots and Dressing Up

During our first spring at Goodsoil there was so much run-off that the Beaver River, immediately south of Goodsoil, flooded its banks and washed out roads including the highway. Many of us from the village drove out to view water rushing through a three-foot wide chasm where the pavement had broken away. We were semi-isolated; southbound travel was the usual way out of the village and in the other direction the road meandered through the park.

With melting of heavy snowfalls there was mud everywhere that spring. When the children went out to play they had to wear rubber boots. One day, Todd came back to the house to tell us Lorie was stuck. Putting on our own boots, Jack and I went out to the yard to investigate. Lorie was crying as she found she was immobile with her little white boots sucked into the mud. She looked pathetic and yet comical. Jack picked her up as her boots remained stationary, and he handed her to me where I stood on dryer ground. He then went back to rescue her little boots.

Todd's first day at school was a special occasion. A few days before, I had walked with both children across the open field and through a bluff of trees to the school. I had taken the opportunity to introduce Todd to his schoolroom. He knew a few of the other children starting in Grade One, and he had even met the teacher and her children. The big day came, and we were all up early. The children and I dressed up, and I took photographs of them before we walked to school.

I enjoyed dressing up the children, but there wasn't often an opportunity to do so. In 1965, Jack was to preside over raising Canada's new maple leaf flag at Goodsoil's Public School. Since he would be wearing his red serge, of course the children and I would dress to fit the occasion. Todd wore a shirt, tie, his best pants and jacket and Lorie wore a pretty dress with her new coat, white shoes and socks. I wore a hat and gloves with my dress, coat and heels. We were surprised that few of the villagers came to the event; school children and their teachers were the main participants, and no one had dressed up.

When I was invited to the Mother's Day Tea hosted by the local Catholic Women's League, I went with the wife of the Co-Op Grocery

Store manager. She was new to the village, and neither of us belonged to the women's group. When we arrived at the tea, we discovered that we were the only women in hats and gloves. We laughed at ourselves, and wondered what the village and farmwomen thought about us that day.

25

Lake Patrol

Our favourite family times were spent at Lac des Isles. I have warm memories of our drives out to the lake. After the day's work and the evening meal, the children and I, and of course Kip, would sometimes go on a security check patrol with Jack. He was still in uniform and would take us in the police car. We were careful to sit in the designated spots dictated by Kip. I sat in front with Lorie on my lap, while Todd sat behind me because Kip always claimed his place directly behind his master. That's where he rode when just the two of them went on patrol, and that's where he rode no matter what. Kip was always upset when the car went off without him, and on those occasions, we had to chain him up until the car was well out of sight.

Once at the lake, dog and children got out to explore while I helped Jack check doors and windows of the rental cabins, closed until the following summer. We'd drive through the campgrounds and cottage subdivision watching for any sign of vandalism, and dreamed of some day owning a cottage ourselves.

We usually walked along the beach, enjoying the quiet beauty of an area deserted for the season. It was a pleasant way to end the day. En route home, Lorie invariably went to sleep in my lap and Jack would carry her into bed where she continued her slumber. Todd always tumbled into bed happily, and quickly went to sleep.

In the summer, Jack would often go on a Sunday afternoon boat patrol. He would take the children and me to the beach before launching the RCMP boat to go about his business with Kip. The children played in the water while I kept a watchful eye. The beach was a popular place for family outings, especially on Sundays, with several families congregated on the sand or at the picnic tables. I was always glad to see the patrol boat approaching after Jack had completed his work. The children and I scrambled into the boat with our towels and picnic lunch.

We enjoyed being out on the water where it was cooler, and when we got to the other side, we would slowly cruise along the shoreline. I loved to sight a loon, to watch ducks trailing their ducklings behind them, and to see lily pads floating on the surface of the water. We would choose a deserted island beach and pull up to shore where we could have an hour or so to ourselves. We'd float and splash about in the water with the children. Kip would dive into the water for sticks we'd throw, and after a mighty shake, he would go off to explore the woods.

We often collected dry wood to build a fire on the sand where we roasted wieners and marshmallows. If there were berries, we'd eat them as we picked. As the sun splashed its last brilliance of the day across the water, we would return to the main beach and prepare for our journey home. We took back wonderful memories of each outing, being all together and close to nature.

Goodsoil's first RCMP detachment opened in a rented house in May 1931. The postmaster provided the constable with meals at the rate of forty cents each.

The Beaver River lies to the south of the village while the Waterhen River and the forest, much of which eventually became the Meadow Lake Provincial Park, are just north of the town site. In the 30's, the area had only rough roads and Indian trails. Police travel was by saddle horse, and in the summer by canoe. One German immigrant and his wife, with a baby on her back, walked the eighty kilometres from the end of the rail line at St. Walburg, to their homestead near Goodsoil. That baby, his son and grandchildren still live on the farm. Homesteaders paid a $10.00 fee for a quarter section of land. New RCMP quarters were built in 1959. Goodsoil remains a bustling village of about 300. The cottage subdivisions are still developing on the shores of popular Lac des Isles as many Goodsoil people return after many years of living and working elsewhere.

26

Losing a Family Pet

In 1966, Jack and I were excited to hear that we were being moved to a Sergeant's point. Promotions were always great news. We would be going to Moosomin, which was a much bigger centre, and there would be new opportunities for us all. We also learned that a new detachment building was to be constructed there; meanwhile, we would live in the quarters next to the office and over the post office. I wasn't looking forward to apartment living downtown with two children and a cat, but I knew we would manage until the new place was ready.

As excited as we were about a bigger centre, there was a downside; we could not take Kip. This beautiful, intelligent animal that had served in three detachments would never adjust to a confined life in an apartment. He needed to have woods and fields to run through when he was not accompanying Jack on patrol. When Jack worked alone those first years on detachment, Kip was sometimes the second man. Just his large, dark presence in the patrol car was enough to deter anyone from taking advantage of his master when his back was turned.

When Jack was working, especially at night, it was something of a comfort for me to know he had Kip with him. When Kip was at home, he watched over the children, let them sit and lie on him, and was patient enough to act as a little cowboy's horse or to pull a little girl's sleigh. When Blackie decided to torment him, he would take her head into his mouth and hold her gently until she stopped teasing. Now we agonized, wondering what to do about this member of our family.

Our hearts were heavy, but the pain was magnified when we tried to explain to the children. They were to leave the only home they both knew, their friends, and now, the family's beloved Kip. This was the first loss in their young lives, and promises of another dog, another time did little to soften the blow.

Jack learned of a middle-aged couple who lived in a remote area south of Meadow Lake. They were looking for a guard dog to live with them beside the service station and coffee shop they operated. Their situation sounded right; Kip would continue living at the edge of the forest where he could roam at will. Our whole family went to deliver

Kip to his new owners. The people were kindly and assured us they would take good care of our pet and working mate. As we walked back to the car, I found myself weeping, despite my earlier resolve, and this did nothing to reassure the children. It was a dark day for our family.

After moving to Moosomin, we received reports of Kip from friends. It seemed he had settled in well and was treated with the respect and affection he deserved. His new owners were known to feed him ice cream cones as a treat when he was on duty in the restaurant and he, in turn, held more than one would-be thief by the arm in his powerful jaws until assistance came.

In our new home, Blackie continued to produce kittens, much to the children's delight. When we moved out of the apartment, we found a small dog for the children, and life went on.

Moosomin, a Cree word for moose berry or cranberry, plentiful in the area, is east of Regina and near the Manitoba border. Some claim the town was named after an old Indian warrior, Chief Moosomin, whose headquarters were somewhere in the Moose Mountains. In 1882, the C.P.R. was built 25 miles south of Fort Ellice and is the site where Moosomin developed. The NWMP set up the first detachment in a tent in 1886. After the brick Post Office was built, the RCMP offices, single men's quarters, and a suite for the in-charge member and his family, were housed on the second floor. In 1968 a new detachment was built on Carleton St. Sgt. Jack Lee-Knight, wife Ruth, and their family were the first occupants of the in-charge quarters. Moosomin's population is 2,403.

27

Lac des Isles Revisited

It was 1975 before we returned to Goodsoil and to camp at Lac des Isles. We enjoyed the lake and woods after renewing old friendships in the village. One incident stands out in my mind when thinking of that time.

During our camping vacation, Jack injured his back. The minor accident sent him seeking relief from a chiropractor at Grande Centre, Alberta, sixty-five miles west. After a couple of treatments and some rest, he was feeling less pain.

One evening, we were relaxing in lawn chairs at our campsite; our young people had taken the car into Goodsoil to visit friends. We could occasionally hear vehicles driving into the cottage subdivision located 300 yards to the northwest. We had heard there was to be an anniversary celebration there. Other than a few voices echoing through the woods from time to time, the campground was quiet.

Nearby, two campers were doing supper dishes at their picnic table, another was roasting marshmallows for his two small children, and an older couple strolled by with their French poodle on a leash.

Jack was organizing his tackle box, and I was lounging with a book I'd brought from the trailer. In time, we became aware of unusual noises coming from the beach area north of the campgrounds. Jack dropped the lures he had been untangling.

"Sounds like someone's messing with the trashcans," he said, as loud clanging echoed through the woods.

"I wonder what all that yelling is about," I said as I sat up and closed my book. We listened for a few more minutes, and when the noises became louder we both stood up. "Someone's up to no good," I said.

"I'm thinking about our boat down there," Jack answered. "Guess I'll stroll over and check things out." I dropped my book and we walked toward the beach. "With that party going on I'm wondering if some kids got into their parents' beer," Jack said.

"Remember, we heard in the village about that habitual vandal living there?" I said. "His parents are the ones having the party."

"Just what I was thinking. Let's stand in that grove of willow and birch so we can have a good view of the beach." We slipped into the stand of trees and watched three teenage boys cavorting along the beach and moving in our direction. One of them was carrying a case of beer. They were yelling and laughing uproariously as they slammed firewood at each trashcan they came upon. One of the youths was kicking a can repeatedly and another clanged lids together like symbols before throwing them into the lake. We knew we had a problem. Before I could think what we should do about it, the trio turned their attention to a boat resting on shore. They threw fishing gear and paddles into the lake, scooped up sand and poured it into the gas tank. They acted like they had been drinking all right.

With heavy boots, one of the boys kicked in the windshield of the second boat. Ours was the next boat in line. Jack tensed beside me. He was about to make a move. I wondered how he could handle three out-of-control teenagers without further injuring his back.

The three would have to pass the grove of trees to get to our boat, and we would be able to jump them from behind, I reasoned to myself. As they passed, Jack burst out of hiding and grabbed at the startled youths. At the same moment, I leapt forward and jumped on the back of one of them.

"The games over, boys," Jack growled. He used their surprise to advantage by getting a firm grip on two of them, but the third wriggled free and ran further down the beach and disappeared into the woods. "Get the rope out of the boat," Jack told me.

I scrambled up, being careful to stay out of the boys' view. I had my own plan. Perhaps they'd settle down if they thought they were up against two men. Darn, no rope in the boat. Doing my best to lower my voice by an octave I answered, "No rope there."

"Untie the one holding the boat to the tree then," was the next command. I knew I had to move quickly as the captives were struggling.

"Okay," I muttered. I ripped at the knot on the boat and again at the end holding it to the tree. My hands were beginning to shake, and I was aware of my heart pounding.

"Please, Mr. Lee-Knight, let us go and we won't do it again," came from one of the captives.

"Here," I barked as I flung one free end of the rope at Jack. I threw a loop around the prisoners with the other end. Jack had the two bound together in seconds.

"Let's move it, boys," he was saying as he led them up from the beach. When they realized their bargaining was falling on deaf ears they started to curse. Following closely behind, I lost my patience with their foul language.

"Watch your mouths," I commanded in my normal voice. Upon hearing me, they hesitated in mid-stride and fell quiet immediately. I believe that was the first moment they realized there was a woman present. They calmed down long enough for us to lead them to the campground where they started to bargain once again.

Our suspicions were right. The ringleader was the notoriously bad actor, the son of the people having the party. He'd simply walked off with the beer while his parents were busy.

As we approached our trailer, I thought, now what? There's no help here and no phone; we don't even have our vehicle. Still, I was glad our children weren't around at the time.

"Get the fellow from the tent beside us," was the next thing I heard, "and get him to drive to the phone and call the detachment in Goodsoil." I hurried to our neighbour as Jack moved his prisoners into the trailer. The fisherman, who'd been up since dawn, had already retired for the night, but he scrambled out of his tent when I called to him about needing help. He drove to the pay phone to call the detachment; soon after, the corporal-in-charge arrived. He drove off with the prisoners as the light faded from the evening sky. Jack added a couple of logs to our dying fire and I sank gratefully into my lawn chair.

As a result of our efforts, the young vandals were barred from the park for the next year.

New detachment quarters in Moosomin in 1968

28

Do We Have To Go?

In 1969, we got word of our transfer from Moosomin to Kamsack. After living in Moosomin for three years, we were happy with our lives. We were in new quarters, had a new dog, new interests, new friends and I was working. We asked one another, "Do we have to go?" We knew what the answer was; we resigned ourselves to another change.

In Kamsack, we settled into the provided quarters, new schools and jobs. The hanging incident during which I assisted the young constable, occurred shortly after building expansion and renovations had taken place in the office portion of the building.

We all learned to love nearby Duck Mountain Provincial Park. The children and I spent a good deal of time there, Jack joining us when he could. We were making friends, and life didn't seem as bleak as we had imagined. Within two years, we discovered we were to move once again.

Kamsack is located at the junction of Highways #8 and #5, close to three Indian Reserves, the Duck Mountain Provincial Park, and is near the Manitoba border. Now called the "Garden of Saskatchewan", the community was settled in the 1880's by Doukhobours, Ukrainians, Europeans, Americans and eastern Canadians. The name Kamsack is a derivative of a Saulteaux word. The population is 2,200. The community has all services including a K-12 school, two museums, a golf course, library, hospital and an airport. There is an RCMP detachment with five urban members and several rural members. The first detachment office was built in 1901.

*Author's daughter Lorie with her father upon arrival at Wollaston Lake
in April, 1972*

29

Move To The City

Our whole family looked forward to moving from detachment quarters to our own home in Prince Albert. It was a four-level split design on a pleasant street and beside a park. For the first time since we had married thirteen years earlier, we had privacy and the freedom to decorate our home as we wanted. The two children attended John Diefenbaker School beyond a hill in the park. They settled in well, as did their pets. All was serene. Before long, however, we discovered Jack would be away from home far more than we had expected.

We knew, as North Section N.C.O., Jack would be flying to several northern points to inspect detachments. His area included Prince Albert City Detachment and ranged as far as Uranium City. Most weeks, he was flown north in an RCMP single Otter, usually on a Monday and would not return until Friday afternoon or evening. There were no telephone facilities in the north, making family contact impossible.

The whole family looked forward to weekends. The house would be tidy and clean, uniform shirts washed and pressed, and a nice meal would be ready each Friday evening. I'd usually visited the hairdresser earlier in the day. After school I'd hear the children making plans.

"Dad's going to make us a rabbit hutch," Lorie said on one occasion.

"That's right. He said he'll take us skiing at Red River Park, too," Todd added.

When their father walked in the door, he'd always get a royal welcome; wife, kids and dog raced to be the first one to greet him. Supper would be a happy time with everyone talking at once, exchanging news and asking questions. We tried to crowd everything we wanted to say and do into two days; we really appreciated that family time.

However, I soon learned to dread the ringing of the telephone near supper hour on Fridays. It generally meant Jack would not be coming home that weekend.

"This is the Radio Room," I'd hear when I'd pick up the phone. "Staff Lee-Knight won't be returning from La Loche (or wherever) this evening. He's storm-stayed." I'd politely thank the radio operator, even though I'd have a lump in my throat. I had to swallow it, put on a happy face and call the children for supper.

"Dad and the pilot can't make it home because it's snowing so heavily it isn't safe." I could barely look at them, knowing the disappointment I'd find there. "We'll just have to put off our plans until next weekend," I'd say breezily. "Want to make popcorn tonight?" I might ask. "You can each ask a friend over." Even though the children were no strangers to disappointment, and even when they appeared to accept what they couldn't change, it was heart breaking for me to know they were silently carrying burdens no child should have to.

One particularly difficult time was when their dog, Toby, went missing. He was last seen on a Sunday evening following the family car when Jack drove Lorie's playmate home. Toby didn't return that night, and, as usual, Jack flew north the next day. Todd and Lorie were very concerned, but I reassured them as best I could.

"Don't worry," I said, trying to sound optimistic. "I'll look for him while you're in school." Later that day I phoned a lost advertisement to the public radio station and placed an ad in the local newspaper. I followed every lead that came, even though I had to drive to unfamiliar areas of the city. It was all to no avail, and I suspected the worst. I kept reassuring the children, "Maybe some kids found him and have him on a leash, so he hasn't been able to find his way home." It became more difficult to field their questions.

On Thursday evening while we were still at the supper table, the phone rang.

"I'm from the City Sanitation Department," the male voice began. "I read your ad and I wanted to let you know I found your dog. I'm sorry to tell you he was killed by a car and was thrown up on a lawn. I kept his collar and license tag if you'd like to have them." My stomach hardened into a tight ball around my supper. I heard details on how to reclaim Toby's collar. As I turned from the phone, I found both children standing nearby, their young faces looking up in anticipation and fear. I could protect them no longer. I put a hand on each of their curly heads.

"Toby's been found dead. A car hit him, but he never knew what happened, so he didn't suffer," was all I could offer before the first sob broke my resolve. We clung to one another, crying over another loss. The children needed their father to help them through this difficult time. I wished I could have, at least, put them in telephone contact with him. That night, the three of us slept in my bed with Fancy, the cat, curled up at our feet. In a few months, Jack presented the children with a darling, black pup that took all our hearts at first sight. We picked up the pieces of our lives once again.

30

A Brush With the Famous

The children enjoyed their school and had made friends quickly. I joined the Stetsonettes, wives of RCMP members. We had an excuse to dress up for our regular dinner meetings or for wine and cheese parties. It gave us all an opportunity for a night out and to share common concerns. Jack and I were able to attend an RCMP Ball without having to leave the city. It was 1973, the year of the RCMP Centennial. Members were called upon to attend many events that year. Jack and I, along with another couple who had square dance experience, lead the grand march for the Provincial Square Dance Association rally. We wore formal attire, and it was quite exciting to lead several hundred square dancers onto the floor.

Another special time was when Todd, Lorie and I were flown by RCMP plane to Regina to attend a ceremony at Depot Division when Queen Elizabeth and Prince Philip were present. My mother, long an admirer of royalty and the Force, joined us. We were dressed in our best, we girls wearing hats and gloves. Even though it was disappointing that Jack was required to remain at Subdivision Headquarters, it was a memorable day for the rest of us.

Another brush with a distinctive personage came for the children and I when John Diefenbaker came to his home riding while we lived in Prince Albert. He was attending a book signing at a local bookstore when his latest publication came off the press. It was snowing heavily and the city streets were slippery that evening, but I didn't want the children to miss meeting Mr. Diefenbaker. I purchased two copies of *The Things We Treasure* and gave one to each of the children before we stood in line. As we drew near to the book-signing desk, I noticed the great gentleman looking tenderly at a baby held by his father.

I heard Mr. Diefenbaker say, "That's one thing I've always regretted in life, that Mrs. Diefenbaker and I never had a family." I was very touched by his sincerity, and his remarks made me realize anew how fortunate I was. When we met him, he signed the books for each of the children, and took time to speak to them in kindly tones. They were very impressed with the experience, and I was happy we had ventured out that wintry night.

As it turned out, we were to meet Mr. Diefenbaker once again. When Jack was eligible for his long-term service medal, and when he was asked whom he would like to make the presentation, he immediately replied, "John Diefenbaker." Arrangements were made and before long our whole family was ushered into his presence at Subdivision Headquarters. I had made a new dress for Lorie, while Todd and I wore our best clothes. Jack, of course, was in red serge. After the brief presentation ceremony, the children and I visited with the important person.

Jack carried in a tray of coffee, juice and dainties. As he walked into the room he hesitated slightly. Mr. Diefenbaker immediately noticed, and without a word, he nodded his head toward me. The moment escaped me entirely, but Jack had suddenly been unsure whom to serve first. The gracious gentleman at once put him at his ease. Our family has fond memories of that day, and we treasure the photographs of the four of us with John Diefenbaker. Two of those photos still hang in our home.

First Nations People knew Prince Albert as "the good wintering place". James Nisbet, a Presbyterian minister, established it as a permanent settlement in 1866. It is located in the rugged forest area on the south bank of the North Saskatchewan River. P. A. was named for Queen Victoria's consort. The city of approximately 34,000 is now known as the "Gateway to the North". Prince Albert National Park is north of the city. The city's crest shows a member of the North West Mounted Policeman with an Indian chief in full headdress. Between them is a beaver, an evergreen tree and wheat sheaves. As the third largest Saskatchewan city, Prince Albert serves as the centre for mining, forestry and agriculture.

31

Time to be a Family

The men who had preceded Jack in his north section N.C.O. position had each stayed the course for only two years. Even after Jack had completed almost three years working in the same position and away from home, there was no indication things were to change. Time was passing us by and we believed it would be grossly unfair if we were never to enjoy a more normal lifestyle before Todd and Lorie were grown up.

With these thoughts in mind, Jack initiated a discussion with his senior officer about creating a change in his circumstances. Even though we were reluctant to leave our comfortable home, we agreed to be transferred anywhere, as long as Jack could be at home a good deal more than he had been. The south section N.C.O. was able to drive to all points he inspected, therefore was able to reach home comparatively easily. We thought it only fair for him and Jack to trade positions, to even out the playing field. At that rate, there would have been no transfer expense incurred, as both families would have remained in their Prince Albert homes. Those responsible apparently didn't consider this option, as we were instead transferred to Swift Current in southwest Saskatchewan.

The first hardship coming from the transfer was the inability to sell our house. It was larger than average and therefore priced higher than most buyers wanted to pay. This situation restricted our choice of homes in Swift Current; we purchased a smaller, less attractive place. Although we made improvements in the house and yard, we were never satisfied. It could not measure up to our recent home. We carried two mortgages for six months.

Todd and Lorie, veterans to moving, found this transfer difficult. At twelve and fifteen, they had reached the vulnerable ages where peer approval is imperative. They discovered it was impossible to be easily accepted by established groups of adolescents, people who had grown up together and who knew nothing about the pain of being outsiders, nor of conforming. Our young people put in many uncomfortable months, but slowly some locals let down their guard enough to get to know and appreciate Todd and Lorie. The Prince Albert house finally sold; we bought our first boat, and made plans to build a cottage. The whole family benefited from Jack being at home more than he was away. We were getting acquainted with neighbours. We all started to relax.

RCMP Single Otter aircraft that flew author's husband to northern detachment points

32

Close Brush With Death

We'd been in Swift Current for one year when the phone rang one pleasant August evening about ten o'clock. The news I received then changed our lives drastically and permanently. It was the O.C. phoning. Without softening the blow, he told me Jack had been in an accident. The impersonal manner in which the message was delivered was more appropriate to being told that my husband would be late for supper. Jack was being taken to Swift Current's airport by road ambulance from Eastend. He was to be flown to University Hospital in Saskatoon. I was badly shaken at the news, and hurt when there was no offer of assistance from this man who lived only a few blocks away. He must have realized I'd be very upset, needing moral support, and perhaps a ride to the airport.

I told Todd and Lorie the news, and added I'd be going with their father. A neighbour would watch over them for me. I had enough presence of mind to phone our family physician who agreed to meet me at the airport to assess Jack's condition. Another neighbour drove me to meet the ambulance.

It was dark by the time the ambulance drove into view. The moment it stopped and an attendant opened the back doors, I peered inside with only the dim interior light to see by. It was very trying to see Jack prostrate on the ambulance stretcher, his face grimacing in pain, apprehension in his eyes. I wiped perspiration from his forehead as I knelt to kiss him. My right hand went automatically to his wrist.

"I'm going to Saskatoon with you," I assured him as I checked his pulse. I wasn't surprised to find it thready and racing. His legs were swathed in layers of absorbent abdominal pads. Even so, blood was oozing through the top layer and saturating the pads under him. The air in the confined quarters of the ambulance was permeated by the scent of perspiration and fresh, coagulating blood. The doctor quickly assessed Jack's condition, and knowing he needed more analgesic, administered intramuscular morphine. Jack's condition was obviously critical; time was of the essence. The air ambulance arrived and he was taken on board. I didn't ask, but I told the attendants I was going to accompany my husband. I was relieved they gave me no argument.

The trip seemed to take a long time. I prayed every moment of it while talking to Jack in a reassuring manner. "It'll be all right," I told him. "We'll be at the hospital soon and they'll take good care of you." I stroked his forehead and hands, not encouraged by his weakening pulse. Finally we landed and Jack had to go through a gruelling transfer from one stretcher to another. At the hospital there was one more transfer. The resident on duty hastily checked the compound fractures of Jack's legs, and he took his vital signs. My body stiffened as I noted the resident having difficulty hearing a blood pressure. A laboratory technician drew blood for cross and match. The resident started an intravenous drip of normal saline. As we came out of the x-ray department, a unit of blood was started in his other arm. I had an overwhelming sense of gratitude to see these first measures administered so efficiently and quickly. I didn't take my eyes off my pain-wracked, haemorrhaging husband until he was wheeled into the operating room.

My sister, Dorothy and her husband Lloyd lived in Saskatoon at the time. I phoned to tell them the news. They were soon at my side, helping me through the difficult waiting. Eventually, I encouraged them to go home, as the next day was a workday. They would have a bed ready for me whenever I decided to leave the hospital; hearing that was a measure of comfort. The night yawned on as I sat in the waiting room coming to grips with the events of the past few hours, imagining what was happening in the operating room, and thinking of the trying times ahead. I prayed for Jack's life to be spared, for him to be returned to his children who had seen so little of him in their young lives.

I sipped coffee without tasting it. The first lights of dawn were creeping up from the horizon when the orthopaedic surgeon walked into the room.

"Your husband made it through the surgery. His legs are quite a mess, and there will be more surgery eventually, but first he has to recuperate from all this shock to his system. We've given him a lot of blood and cleaned up his wounds. He's sleeping, but you can go in to see him for a minute." I thanked the surgeon as tears sprang to my eyes and my legs suddenly felt wobbly. Somehow, I made it to the recovery room. It was a great relief to see Jack's relaxed features and normal colour. His respirations were slow and even, his pulse strong and regular. I was aware of my own muscles loosening as I drew in my first deep breath of the night. At that point, I told myself, since we'd made it this far, we'd make it all the way.

33

Long Road to Recovery

For Jack, the next several weeks consisted of pain, injections, dressing changes, and general hospital routine. He had dozens of friends and acquaintances visit him; so many, that we started a guest book for signatures and addresses. Every one had read the newspaper account of his accident. It was some days after that dreadful night before I heard all the facts from Jack.

He had finished inspections of the Shaunavon and Eastend detachments, and was preparing to return home. When he became aware that a young Eastend member was having problems and needed someone to talk to, he decided to stay there for supper. He would spend time with the member, help sort out his problems before driving home late. I knew that to be typical of Jack. Once on the highway, dusk was deepening, and as he drove on, he noticed someone stranded on the side of the road. Realizing it was a woman alone, he turned back to inquire if he could be of help; another typical characteristic. When he discovered her engine had a loose fan belt, he thought he'd try to fix it himself sooner than radio for a service man to drive out. This was his third helpful, but almost fatal, decision of the evening.

He drove onto the shoulder of the road with his headlights directed into the engine of the other car. He had fixed the fan belt when it slipped off again. Concentrating on the task at hand, he was unaware of a third car speeding toward him. The owner of the stranded vehicle did not warn Jack of the danger he was in, but leapt to safety into the ditch as the rear of her car was slammed into, pinning Jack between it and the police cruiser. Gravely injured, bleeding heavily and in shock, Jack struggled to remain conscious. He tried to explain to the woman whom he had been helping, how to use the police radio. He knew his life depended on getting help quickly. She couldn't seem to follow his instructions.

Out of desperation, he dragged himself slowly and painfully to the car door. He was unable to reach the radio. Time was passing and light was fading from the evening sky. Finally, with one last heroic effort, Jack heaved his upper body onto the car seat. When he reached the radio, he discovered the woman had moved the controls to all the wrong settings. It was almost impossible for his shaking hands to make the subtle adjustments the dials required. Eventually, he was able to make radio contact. A police car and an ambulance finally came to his rescue.

The drunk driver of the other car sustained only a cut lip. As it happened, she continued her drinking habits until, some years later, she killed herself and two others in another motor vehicle accident.

I divided my time between the University Hospital in Saskatoon and being at home with the children. Those weeks became a blur of memories. I drove back and forth between the two cities, something I'd never done before, and I learned the route to my sister's home, having never driven in Saskatoon. I handled most of the responsibilities Jack had always considered his. It was vital I be with him, especially during the early post-operative weeks. He needed all my loving care, support and encouragement to keep his spirits up, and in so doing, contribute to his healing. I wanted to be with him, and yet I was I worried about Todd and Lorie at home.

My mother was able to stay with them for a short while, but basically they were on their own, getting their meals, looking after the dog, answering the door and phone, often calls from people inquiring about their father. Whenever I went home for a few days, there was a flurry of activity. I caught up with the laundry, cleaned house, bought groceries, made freezer meals and baked, paid bills, did the banking, and sorted through accumulating mail.

I'd be back in Saskatoon, hardly remembering the highway trips, my mind being with Jack and with Todd and Lorie. I was so proud of the way the children handled themselves during that very trying period. I'm sure they both silently gave up more and suffered more than we'll ever know.

Jack struggled through many difficult weeks in physical therapy, regaining strength and eventually learning a stiff-legged gait with both legs encased in plaster from his toes to his groins. When he was to be released from hospital, I made a number of preparations to accommodate his new situation. Bars were installed at the back steps, in the bathroom, next to his recliner chair in the living room and beside our bed. The whole family made adjustments of various kinds, but the important thing was we were all together again. It was a profound relief for Jack to be at home, and for us to have him there.

Because winter was closing in, we were glad the car trips were over. Jack was to practice walking, and because he needed fresh air and a change of scenery, we went out once a day. There was too much snow on the sidewalks, therefore he accomplished his slow, stiff steps on the road with one of the children on one side and me supporting him on the other. I prayed he wouldn't topple over, as I didn't know how well we'd be able to steady his two hundred and fifty pounds plus the added plaster weight. I also prayed no speeders came our way.

Over the next several months, the casts were replaced and reduced in size. We assumed the bones were healing, but Jack's continuing pain was a concern. Late the next summer, it was discovered the bones in his left leg had not healed. Bone grafting surgery was scheduled. There was another round of surgery, intense pain, analgesic injections, recuperation, and physical therapy. It was important for Jack not to lose hope. It was up to me to help him maintain a positive attitude. It was a happy day when we were told the bone grafting had been successful.

After a period of rest at home, surgery for skin grafting was scheduled. Jack returned to Saskatoon for the procedure and for weeks of healing time. Two years went by before he was declared fit to work. He would not be travelling any longer, but would take a position in Swift Current Subdivision office, as the Subdivision N.C.O. It was a dreamed-of change for the children and me to have their father with us every evening and weekend, something most people, even some RCMP families take for granted. We were finally together; we were a family.

The City of Swift Current, deriving its name from the creek that runs through it, is in southwest Saskatchewan. The C.P.R. reached Swift Current and bridged the creek in 1882. It is reported that the last buffalo killed in the area took place in 1887 and 1888. Many settlers took up ranching of cattle and sheep. The "76 Ranch", a huge cattle operation in the area, branded all its cattle with "76". Many young men coming from England to work for the "76 Ranch" eventually took up land and established their own ranches.

In 1884 Treaty #4 was signed in the area in the presence of NWMP members who had arrived after their march from Manitoba. Today the City of Swift Current is policed by the RCMP. Presently there is a complement of twenty regular and ten civilian members supervised by a Staff Sergeant. The rural area is covered by ten regular members and three civilians supervised by two Sergeants.

Swift Current is known for forming the first Health Region in Saskatchewan. Oil was discovered in several locations in the Swift Current district in the 1950's and greatly contributed to the city's economy.

34

Life After Jack's Accident

It took a life-threatening accident to give our children a full-time father. It was special for our son and daughter to have him available to attend their sports events and to become involved in many aspects of their lives. I was relieved to place most of our affairs back into his capable hands. With life taking on at least a modicum of normalcy, I was able to return to nursing. I worked part time at first before eventually taking a full-time position.

Jack would never regain his pre-accident energy; nor would he be completely free of pain. His skin grafts were very tenuous and tended to break down easily. Their location on his shins made them vulnerable to injury. For years, I closely watched these areas, cleansing injuries and changing dressings as required. Infection was a constant threat, especially if it should spread to the bone grafts below.

We had always loved to dance, and although we slowly resumed a social life, each dancing attempt resulted in a few days of extra pain. Biking and hiking were two of our hobbies, but these were permanently reduced to an occasional spin or stroll around the block. Although I still walk and bike, it is never as enjoyable doing so without my husband.

After serving the Force for thirty-four years, Jack retired. He was then able to spend more time on his many hobbies, and to do volunteerism, especially within our church and for the RCMP Veterans' Association. He has always made it a priority to visit hospitalized friends.

I had retired a year earlier, so was able to devote more time to writing and to being involved with writers' groups. Reading, gardening and volunteerism also take up much of my time. We enjoy spending our summers together at our cottage, and sometimes visiting warm countries in the winter. Being with our family, including two grandchildren, is always special for us.

Life has dealt us many and varied cards, some heart wrenching and destructive, others joyful and fulfilling. Regardless, we faced each new day together and supported one another, no matter what.

Again, I am reminded of that Biblical quote:

> ... *for I want to go wherever you go,*
> *and to live wherever you live;*
> *your people shall be my people,*
> *and your God shall be my God ...*

> *Ruth 1:16*

35

Awakening to History

While living in Onion Lake in the early 1960's, I had sometimes waited for the ferry on the banks of the North Saskatchewan River, and had many times driven through Fort Pitt. I was not then fully aware of the dramatic events that had occurred in these settings circa 1885. The Frog Lake Massacre and its ramifications had involved a large area of northwest Saskatchewan. I recognized the massacre as history; however, when living at Onion Lake, my immediate concerns caring for my family, and being involved in detachment activities, pushed it to the background. When I had viewed the cairn that had been unveiled by William Bleasdell Cameron, the sole male survivor of the massacre, sympathy stirred in me. I didn't, however, wish to linger in the wild and lonesome area where the base of the cairn was overgrown with grass and weeds.

Some years later, curiosity led me to read Cameron's book, *Blood Red the Sun*. My interest was captured. I found it compelling to contemplate the cairn's unveiling which had taken place only thirty-seven years before I had first viewed it, when I was unable to appreciate the full extent of its importance. I read with interest, that the speaker at the unveiling had been Rev. Edward Ahenakew, an Indian and an ordained clergyman of the Church of England. According to Cameron, the eloquent address was not an apology. It was a plea for charity and understanding of the red man and his feelings that had ultimately led to the horrendous deed.

When we had moved to Onion Lake in April of 1962, I later realized it was the same month, seventy-seven years earlier, in which the Massacre had occurred. Frog Lake, only a short drive across the Saskatchewan/Alberta border, was then part of the Onion Lake Detachment area. It was often the extensive policing required at Frog Lake that was responsible for many nights I spent worried and alone.

Frequent calls, from the reserve or Métis colony reporting disturbances or complaints, had required investigation and action by the RCMP. My husband was usually alone when he visited the Frog Lake area, and often his presence was required there during the night. I had been concerned about the number of people he might have to deal with at one time, especially when liquor was involved and where tempers could flare. It had not helped me to relax when I learned about one occasion when the coil was removed from the patrol car's motor while Jack was inside the Frog Lake Hall sorting out that night's problems.

At such times, I used to speculate about circumstances leading to the Massacre and about the natives who had murdered innocent people. Further research in later years helped me to imagine some of the hardships endured by the Frog Lake band members, and how one group felt they had to take matters into their own hands.

Subsequently, I came to understand something of the wretched suffering inflicted on the only two white women at Frog Lake in 1885. Mrs. Theresa Delaney from Aylmer, Ontario was the wife of farming instructor, John Delaney, and Mrs. Theresa Gowanlock of Parkdale, Ontario was the wife of John Gowanlock. He had established a saw mill at Frog Lake which provided employment for several men, Indians included. The women had witnessed the murder of their husbands and other men. Cameron's book describes how the natives had dragged the white women through coarse brush and sloughs, tearing their clothes and flesh. Although they had suffered intensely, the women's grief and terror had rendered them insensitive to pain. Eventually they were separated and pushed into tents.

According to Cameron's book, Mrs. Gowanlock later said, "The squaws inside noticed I was shaking with cold and took off my shoes and dried them and offered me something to eat." A half-breed interpreter, Mr. Pritchard, purchased the two women to save them from further degradation. Cameron writes that Mrs. Gowanlock also said, "Big Bear frequently came to see us. Mr. Pritchard would interpret. The chief professed sorrow, telling us it was the fault of his braves whom he could not control."

Another man responsible for securing the purchase of the women from the Indians was Adolphus Nolin, a half-breed, who later lived on a ranch near Onion Lake. Seventy-seven years later, his great-grandchild became a playmate to my small son. I became acutely aware of the thin line of history, however convoluted, connecting my family to the grim drama of Northwest Saskatchewan.

When I had first heard the Onion Lake name, *Kahneepotaytayo*, pronounced and written for ease, *Canapotato*, I was amused. I would have been more suitably impressed had I known the name descended from the man who had been head dancer of Chief Big Bear's band of Plains Cree. According to Cameron, this man had been a marvellous performer in the War Dance and in other dancing ceremonies. He had later lived on the Onion Lake Reserve. One of his wives was the daughter of Wandering Spirit, who was a murderer and notorious instigator of the Massacre. Another wife was a daughter of *Apischiskoos*, who was one of the murderers hanged at Battleford.

It was April 14, 1885, forty-nine years to the day before my husband was born, when Big Bear had dictated a letter to Sergeant Martin of the North West Mounted Police. Big Bear, still having difficulty in controlling his men, spoke of his friendship with the Sergeant and of his gratefulness for the good blanket given to him and for other favours. He had urged the Sergeant to evacuate with his troop immediately in order to avoid any bloodshed. It was apparent Big Bear knew he could not hold his wild men much longer.

Years later, I strolled across the site of historic Fort Pitt trying to picture the pilfering scene unfolding, as told in Cameron's book. An engraved watch, worn by Charles Dickens and bequeathed to his son, Captain Francis J. Dickens had been stolen, but the Captain eventually recovered this special memento. An eyewitness to the looting reported how the Indians took everything in sight. Sugar, tea, tobacco, and calico were seized while containers of pickled walnuts and pate de foie gras were sniffed at and thrown away. All the medicines were consumed on the spot.

From the perspective of seventy-seven years later, it was difficult to envision this drama on the quiet, abandoned plains of Fort Pitt. It was almost as hard to imagine 1885 steamboats from Edmonton docking on the North Saskatchewan River at Fort Pitt before going on to Battleford.

When I read of those steamboats, I recalled how we had often taken our car across the same river. I marvelled at the incredible history that had taken place on and near this river. My thoughts again returned to the women captives. I eventually read of their trying experiences as chronicled in their book *Two Months in Big Bear's Camp*. Their book also shares the gratitude they always felt for those that helped them, and for Big Bear's obvious concern for their welfare.

Since researching Big Bear's history, I hold great respect for him. I also feel deep empathy for the situation in which he found himself. I believe it is regrettable this great leader was sentenced to jail for a crime he did not commit. Equally lamentable is his eventual death from what appears to have been a broken heart.

Over forty years ago, I found our Onion Lake posting a trying one, and as anxious as I was to leave, I appreciate how that experience has ultimately piqued my interest in Saskatchewan's history and history of all kinds.

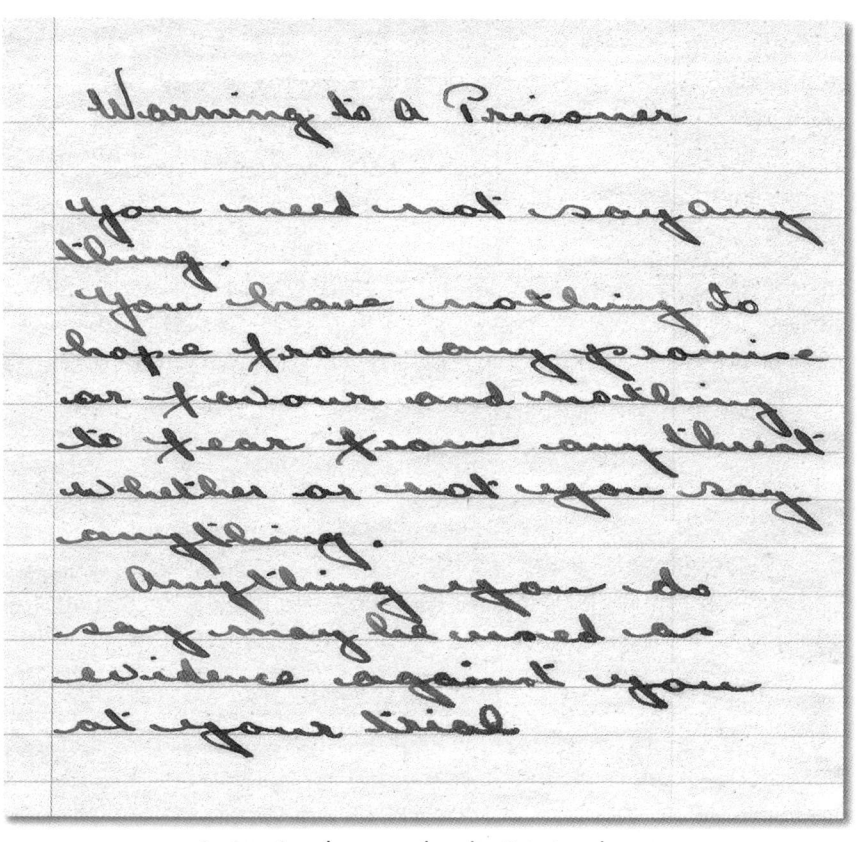

Instructional notes taken by E.A. Jewsbury
during Criminal Code of Canada classes, circa 1930

Author's father, E.A. Jewsbury, circa 1930

Stained glass window of Biblical Ruth in RCMP chapel, Regina

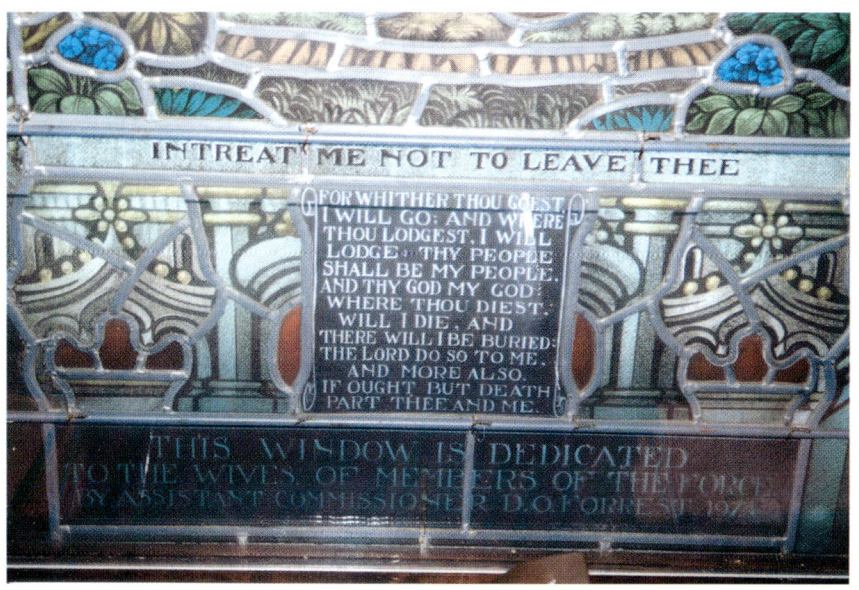

Text on stained glass window.
Dedicated to the wives of members of the force

Cairn and grave site at Frog Lake, Alberta

HISTORIC SITES and MONUMENTS BOARD of CANADA

NORTH WEST REBELLION.

FROG LAKE MASSACRE.

HERE ON 2ND APRIL, 1885,
REBEL INDIANS UNDER
BIG BEAR MASSACRED

REV. FATHER LÉON ADÉLARD FAFARD, O.M.I.,
REV. FATHER FÉLIX MARCHAND, O.M.I.,
INDIAN AGENT THOMAS QUINN,
FARM INSTRUCTOR JOHN DELANEY,
JOHN ALEXANDER GOWANLOCK,
WILLIAM CAMPBELL GILCHRIST,
GEORGE DILL,
CHARLES GOUIN,
JOHN WILLISCROFT.

THEY TOOK PRISONERS
MRS. THERESA DELANEY,
MRS. THERESA GOWANLOCK.

Text on cairn at Frog Lake

Bride and groom, author and husband at Humboldt, 1958

Author's children with Blackie, Goodsoil, 1964

Cattle drive passing detachment, Onion Lake, 1963

Cattle breaking in, Onion Lake, 1963

Author's children, Lorie 2nd from right front, and Todd at right back, Goodsoil, 1965

Todd the cowboy, Goodsoil, 1965

Todd's first day of school with Lorie and the bear rug, Goodsoil, 1965

Lee-Knight family with John Diefenbaker, 1973

Author, Rt., with mother and daughter Lorie in front of RCMP chapel, Regina, 1973

The Officer Commanding
and members of the Prince Albert Subdivision
Royal Canadian Mounted Police
request the pleasure of your company at their

Centennial Ball

Friday, May Twenty-fifth, Nineteen Hundred and Seventy-three
at the Prince Albert Recreation Centre

COCKTAILS 7 - 8:30 p.m.	BUFFET DINNER 8:30 p.m.	DANCING 10:00 - 2 a.m.
ADMISSION BY	RECEIVING LINE	DRESS FORMAL
INVITATION ONLY	7:45 TO 8:15 p.m.	REFRESHMENTS

Centennial Ball invitation and coaster, 1973

THE COMMISSIONER
ROYAL CANADIAN MOUNTED POLICE
Requests the Honour of Your Presence at Special Ceremonies

ON THE PARADE SQUARE
Royal Canadian Mounted Police
"Depot" Division, Regina, Saskatchewan.
Between the hours of 9:45 A.M., and 12:00 Noon

WEDNESDAY, JULY 4, 1973

HER MAJESTY THE QUEEN AND HIS ROYAL HIGHNESS
THE DUKE OF EDINBURGH WILL BE PRESENT.

Guests must be seated by 9:45 A.M.

This Invitation must be presented for admittance.

Invitation to see the Queen at Depot Division, Regina, 1973

Queen Elizabeth and Prince Philip on the RCMP Parade Square, Regina, 1973

36

Sisters in the Service

During the years that we were stationed at one-man or two-man detachments, I rarely had contact with wives in a similar situation to mine. Often there was considerable distance between detachments; travel between them was seldom considered for purely social visits.

Detachment men were able to visit during the course of their duties. They sometimes made a "meet" on the highway halfway between their detachments, and often conducted investigations jointly. On occasion, a member visited another detachment en route to Subdivision.

Our husbands often worked around the clock and almost never took a day off, but they enjoyed one another's company whenever they had the opportunity to meet. Coffee breaks and meals at roadside service stations or at a detachment home provided the contact they needed with fellow officers. They were, after all, detached from their comrades in bigger centres.

While they were detached, we wives suffered more from isolation; we were deprived of our families and friends. It was not always possible for wives to make close friends in the short time we were stationed at one location. As a result, we wives could spend lonely months caring for our family and homes while rarely seeing other people.

It was uncommon for a detachment wife to leave her busy husband to go home for a visit with relatives and friends. In my case, the distance involved was often too great, and given the desolate country I would have had to drive through, there would have been considerable risk. If I'd had a problem on the road, there would have been no help available for too many miles.

Besides, I knew my absence would have made my husband's job more difficult. He needed hot meals that could be served quickly when he was pressed for time. He needed clean uniforms, and it helped having me answer the phone and take messages when he was grabbing a few hours sleep after a long night patrol. We were a team, and I stayed the course.

When I was spending so much time alone, I sometimes wondered how other wives coped. I knew that some were stationed closer to family, and others lived in larger communities. There were some two-man detachments where both men were married. I considered such wives to be extremely lucky. Regardless of our particular circumstances, we experienced much the same lifestyle and performed many of the same tasks in order to lighten our husbands' heavy loads. We were sisters in the service.

As I lived my detachment dramas, others lived theirs. "Herstories" came long before mine, and for a few years after, there were others. What follows are "herstories" as told to me.

37

Settling in at Stony

Florence and Frank Wilson with their two children were scheduled to move from Wakaw, Saskatchewan to Stony Rapids at the end of June, 1973. Due to a huge forest fire threatening the community, and burning to the edge of the schoolyard, their transfer was delayed until July 21st. It was a 90-degree, windy, dusty day when they landed at the sandy airstrip. Florence's first impression was that they were landing on a desert. There was no village in sight.

A vehicle arrived to transport them to their new detachment. They were unable to unpack until the departing family left. Florence was relieved when she was finally able to settle in.

Basic furniture, dishes and cooking utensils were supplied. Florence had taken her pressure cooker and linens. She had also taken materials and her sewing machine which she came to think of as her lifesaver. She spent many nights sewing when Frank was working and the children were in bed. Letter writing to family and friends became another pastime when she found herself alone.

Florence vividly recalls the first blueberry season after her arrival in Stony, as everyone there refers to the village. She often took her children, eighteen-month-old Rob, and Karen who was three, to look for berries. Little by little they ventured off the side of the road, but not far enough to get lost, or before getting too tired to walk home. She eventually had a good supply of berries stored in the freezer. The following year, she felt braver and went off berry picking alone, leaving the children with their dad whenever possible.

Early in October that first year, CF-MPW, the RCMP plane, was at Stony. Florence decided to take the opportunity to fly to Prince Albert on its return trip. She knew she wouldn't be able to "get out" until the following spring, so she bundled up the two children who were anxious to go to visit their grandmother in Yorkton. The family car was in storage in Prince Albert, so after retrieving it, they drove as far as Wakaw to spend the night. They travelled on to Yorkton and spent a week visiting. Florence then took her family back to Prince Albert and stayed overnight. They, along with their care packages from Grandmother, boarded MPW early the next morning.

With winter approaching, daylight hours were shortened. It was not unusual for darkness to descend in mid-afternoon. Because Florence had a lot of time on her hands, she made a couple of quilts while living at Stony. She remembers her son being so proud of his new quilt. When Inspector Tom Light was visiting the detachment, Rob took the quilt off his bed and dragged it out to show what his mom had made. Florence still has the quilt, even though it's getting a little tattered.

Florence spent a lot of time outdoors with the children. Often they'd be tobogganing in twenty below weather. She was glad the children were very young while they were stationed at Stony. She looked forward to them having better opportunities once they were transferred again.

Florence was alone quite often when Frank was away on two or three day patrols to Wollaston or Fond-du-Lac. The Fond-du-Lac River ran by only a few yards from the front of the detachment property, and when Florence looked from the living room window, she could see a fair distance. She thought she would wear a path in the floor from east to west watching for a glimpse of Frank coming home by boat in the summer or on a skidoo in the winter.

Baking all the bread and buns occupied several hours every week. The baking always turned out well when it was just for the family; there were other times when the crusts fell off the buns. That seemed to happen only when she had guests for a meal at inspection time. Florence was a little embarrassed serving them, but the guests did their best to make her feel they were okay.

She remembers being invited out for a meal on a houseboat. Outfitters from Iowa operated the houseboat, taking tourists on fishing trips. This was a special treat for her and a change from her own cooking.

Feeding prisoners was one of her duties at Stony. Florence was surprised to find them fussy eaters. For one thing, they didn't like sardines. She served them to the prisoners whenever her family was having them. When there were prisoners to feed, she just made up a bigger supply of the family's meal.

Florence recalls going to a food wholesaler before moving up to Stony. They bought canned food by the case lots as they were advised. To this day, neither Frank nor Florence ever buy turkey noodle soup. She reports they had a "gut full" after finishing the case.

One time, Florence had a welcome break from her lonely winter stretch. She had the opportunity to accompany Frank on a charter to Wollaston Lake when he had a few hours of police work to attend to. As it turned out, the trip involved her acting as stenographer for an inquest into the drowning death of a local fishermen. She was the only one in the area who had some experience with shorthand and so was summarily pressed into service. It was a change of scenery for her, and she saw a few sled dog teams working out.

Florence was quite surprised to discover the police radio was located in the detachment living room. She remembers one particular evening when Frank was away, a message was being transmitted to the detachment. She could tell the radio operator was trying to contact Stony, and he could obviously hear her, but she couldn't make out the message. The operator tried for hours but it was no use. The next day, the airwaves cleared and the message was received. It was about Frank's father from Vancouver who was having surgery for cancer.

Some years later, Florence asked Rob what he remembered about living at Stony. His reply was, "The time Dad lost his sunglasses when they fell overboard while on a boat ride." It seems he recalled his Dad's choice of words when that happened.

Florence remembers Karen pushing a broom along the sidewalk ahead of her, when the broom handle jabbed her in the mouth. She was fortunate not to lose any teeth, but there was blood all over. Frank was not around, so Florence grabbed her, and with Rob in tow, headed downhill, then uphill to the nurse's station. Karen bawled all the way while half the village of inquisitive native children followed them. After getting her all cleaned up, Florence wondered why she had panicked.

Another time, Rob received a gash on the back of his head as he fell while jumping on his bed. Frank happened to be at the detachment, so he drove Rob to the nursing station where he had four or five stitches to close the gap.

Florence remembers being worried about the furnace. There were times when it would wind up, building up the combustion for a long period, and then it felt like it would blow the house apart when it started to release some heat. No one believed her, since it never worked that way when her husband was at home. The first time she experienced the furnace problem was around bedtime for the children, and Frank was out of town. She feared for their safety, so with the children in pyjamas, she carried Rob, and with Karen in tow, they travelled up the hill to the schoolteacher's place. She asked him to check the furnace. She was obliged to walk as she had no "wheels" at her disposal. Another night Florence was reading to the children in the living room when the furnace started acting up. Rob became worried and said to his mother, "Mom, let's go in the bedroom and cry."

During the winter, there were only about thirteen white people in the community. There were no playmates for the Wilson children at Stony. The white population included pilots and their wives with Calm Air and Norcan Air. There were a few teachers and their spouses, a nurse, and Department of Natural Resources personnel. Once in a while, the group had a movie night, taking turns hosting the evening. Buckets full of popcorn always went with the event. Occasionally, the Wilsons went by boat or police car to Black Lake to visit a teaching couple and their children. Once spring arrived and the fishing lodges opened for tourists, the population of Stony grew.

The highlight of Florence's stay at Stony was when Commissioner and Mrs. Nadon of Ottawa came to do some fishing. While the members put the office in good order, Florence made sure her house was clean and tidy. The Wilsons were advised that no meal was required for their visitors since they would have their lunch at Uranium City before flying to Stony. Florence served coffee and fresh blueberry pie before the men went fishing. Unfortunately, the weather turned cool and rainy, and no fish could be found.

While the men were out on the water, Mrs. Nadon visited with Florence and the children. Florence was nervous before the visit, but her visitor seemed to be down to earth, and they spent the time chatting about their experiences with the Force. It wasn't until after the Nadons had left, that Florence discovered the meal at Uranium City had never materialized. She felt badly, as had she known, she would have prepared a meal. At any rate, Florence was pleased to receive a letter from Mrs. Nadon thanking her and Frank for their hospitality.

Exactly two years after their arrival, the Wilson family left Stony Rapids. It was as hot a day as on their arrival when they boarded the Twin Otter with their "kit and caboodle". They flew to Yorkton for their next posting.

Following retirement from the Force, Florence and Frank Wilson settled in Watrous, Saskatchewan where, for many years, they owned and operated The Watrous Manitou, a weekly newspaper. They are now enjoying retirement in Watrous. Frank is an award winning artist and he supplied the cartoon illustrations for this book.

Stony Rapids is a charming community located along the rushing Fond-du-Lac River that is just south of the Northwest Territories. Recently, a road has been opened to link the community of 250 to the rest of the north. The very busy airport has regularly scheduled flights, and many bring in fishermen and hunters for world famous sports-fishing and game hunting.

38

Well Married

Shirley and Guy Marcoux were married for over fifty years, but they had a rough beginning. She was an English Protestant schoolmarm marrying a French Canadian Roman Catholic, with parents on both sides strongly objecting. The French Canadian parents "drove hell-bent across Canada to be present for the wedding". Saskatchewan skies welcomed them with heavy rains resulting in gumbo roads. In spite of all these problems, love prevailed and the little United Church blessed the uniting of two cultures on July 9, 1955."

Since Shirley and Guy were wed in a Protestant church, their vows were not recognized in the eyes of the R.C. church until such time as there was another ceremony by the bishop. Consequently, the newlyweds spent their wedding night in a motel, with Guy in a room with his father, and Shirley in another room with her mother-in-law. The two women were unable to communicate as one woman spoke only French and the other spoke English exclusively. Shirley's aunt had "kindly" stitched the bottom of her nightgown closed. In darkness, and with tears running down her cheeks, the bride silently tried to rip and pick the stitches out. After all, one didn't go to bed in the nude with a new mother-in-law.

Because an appointment with the bishop was a week away, they decided to take in the Calgary Stampede, all four of them. They enjoyed the Stampede, returned to Saskatoon to be doubly wed, and began their married life. In the end, both sets of parents accepted their chosen mate and loved them dearly.

A posting to the Village of Imperial, Saskatchewan came shortly thereafter. Moving day was quite an experience. In those days, members had to do all the packing and unpacking themselves. When the Marcoux couple arrived at their new home, it was overflowing with members from other nearby detachments, and there were local farmers and businessmen providing unloading assistance. Of course, there was socializing; this was a first lesson in the spirit of togetherness among members of the Force.

The Marcoux combined house and detachment office was a huge affair. It had a bathroom with a cistern in the basement to provide the water. Since the water was not drinkable, they had drinking water delivered to a big barrel in their kitchen. The local waterman's idea of sanitation left much to be desired. In the winter, Shirley shuddered to see him wiping his runny nose on his sleeves as he filled their barrel. Boiling water became a priority.

Feeding prisoners was a very common duty for detachment wives. There was a high-spirited Irish family living in the next village, and they kept the RCMP occupied with their activities of rustling cattle, fighting within the family, and drinking as much as was available. These were only a few of their tricks. Joe, the oldest one, frequently kept Shirley company in the kitchen, bouncing her baby son on his knee while she made lunch, and while Joe awaited transport to the Regina jail. Shirley was often rewarded for feeding Joe, as he supplied her with garden vegetables when he was free in the community again.

Visits from the Subdivision Non-Commissioned Officer and even the Officer Commanding were quite frequent, especially in the fall when duck season was in full bloom near Long Lake. This entailed early morning breakfasts of bacon and eggs.

"I guess the local restaurant must have been located in my kitchen," Shirley said.

One incident she well remembers when her son was very young, and she was sitting in the front room nursing him. The Staff/Sergeant came into the room to visit, and she was very embarrassed to be so occupied. Some years later, Shirley thought of how greatly times have changed.

Another Staff/Sergeant used to visit, and while he was doing his inspection, he would tell Shirley to take off for the lake with the detachment police car. The men would join her later for a picnic supper.

"Just toss a blanket over the crest on the car door," he would say. He was one of Shirley's favourites.

Her husband had jokingly, Shirley thinks, told the Subdivision N.C.O. that if he was left in Imperial long enough, he would fill the house with kids. Perhaps the N.C.O. believed him, because after two and a half years and two children, they were transferred to New Brunswick.

Shirley and Guy eventually moved into the corporal's apartment above the office of a five-man detachment. As a general rule, coffee break took place around the Marcoux dining room table, and Shirley usually had cookies or cake available. One member used to tell her that she made the best soggy chocolate cake he had ever tasted. She took it as a compliment.

Their apartment was a good size, so the socials for members and wives were often held in the Marcoux home. "Those were the good old days of little money but lots of fun," Shirley said. There were BYOB (Bring Your Own Bottle) parties, and Shirley has warm and wonderful memories of good and lasting friendships.

One holiday season, her youngest sister came to visit, and she was the instigator of the following incident. Fatigue duty, or office cleaning, was scheduled for Friday afternoons. All members pitched in to scrub, wax and polish the floors, and once the office sparkled, it was well-earned time for TGIF (Thank God It's Friday). One Friday, the purchase of a bottle of rye had been made in advance, and it sat on Shirley's kitchen counter.

Some of the wives had dropped in for coffee, and it was suggested they pull a trick on the fellows. With great care and much laughter, they lifted the foil, removed the cap, and poured the rye into an empty container before refilling the bottle with cold tea. The cap and foil were carefully replaced, and no sign of tampering could be seen. In due course, the bottle was taken to the single men's quarters to be enjoyed.

The wives missed the next episode, but they subsequently learned the tasters were righteously indignant and disappointed to discover tea instead of rye. Off to the Liquor Store went a couple of the members, to complain about such a dirty trick. They were mollified by receipt of a fresh bottle, along with profuse apologies on the part of the Liquor Store staff. The wives were aghast to realize their trick had gone so far. It was some weeks before they finally dared confess to their husbands where the real guilt lay.

The end of detachment life came for Shirley and Guy when they were transferred to Campbellton, New Brunswick in 1958.

It is regrettable that Shirley passed away before seeing her story in print.

"Jeez, Riley, smarten up! There's th' Corporal's wife ..."

39

Leader and Other Points of Interest

One of Gerri Madill's first recollections about Leader was regarding a missing man. He hadn't been seen for approximately three days when his family reported his disappearance. He was a chronic alcoholic, and the family was accustomed to him being a few days late returning from the farm to the town where he lived.

Gerri's husband, Doug, was the only member present at the detachment, as one member was on holidays and the other was away on days off. Doug had had very little sleep for a few days investigating the matter and utilizing many community resources to search the area. He had come in very late on the one night and was sleeping in at 9:00 a.m. The missing person's son-in-law went to the Madill's front door, which nobody used, and demanded to talk with Doug. When Gerri got to the bedroom to wake Doug up, this man was right behind her at the bedside. She asked him to return to the door and to wait there for Doug.

Understandably, the family was upset but, as it turned out, the real reason they wanted the person located, was that they did not want to wait seven years to have him declared legally dead. To this date, neither the body nor the truck the man was driving have been located. That was over twenty years ago.

One busy Saturday afternoon in Leader, Gerri was going shopping. Being quite new to the town, she did not know many people. However, many knew who she was. The Madills had only one child at the time, and Gerri was pushing him in the stroller. As they approached an intersection, a car pulled up to the curb and parked, blocking a fire hydrant. The two young fellows got out of their vehicle and started to walk into a store. They looked at Gerri, went back to their vehicle and moved it immediately. She had no idea who they were, but suspected they knew she was a policeman's wife. She believed that was their motivation for changing their parking from illegal to legal.

Gerri remembers that Doug never had weekends off in Leader, and basically worked day shifts only when he was temporarily in charge. They made some good friends there who were prepared to socialize, play cards and board games during the week. They tended to start the evenings early, as they all had to work the next day, but they went late anyhow.

"Next time you send those two young constables out back to change a tire on the police car, let me know so I can find some ear plugs for these two yahoos ..."

They also had excellent parties at Christmas time. The party would be during the week so that all three members could attend. They had a few friends in common and each member invited two or three other couples. They would break into small groups and put on skits or performances to entertain the whole group. It was great fun, even though the teams would go into all areas of Gerri's house looking for props for their skits (even nightgowns). There were always friends to help clean up. Family life was good, partly because Gerri was not working, and all their other activities could be planned around Doug's work schedule.

Leader is located northwest of Swift Current, near the Alberta border. Immigrants were mainly Germans from Russia. They named their new community Prussia, but during World War I, they changed it to Leader. The earliest record of RNWMP in the area was in June, 1907. The town that has been policed by the Force since 1907, presently has a three-man contingent. The town's population is 1,000. Leader has a large agricultural district and, because it lies directly in migratory bird flyways, it is a popular hunting area.

When the Madills lived at Onion Lake, their residence was next to the detachment. The driveway, in which the police vehicles were parked, was adjacent to their front yard where the children would play. One summer evening while the boys, ages three and four, were playing in the bathtub, Gerri went into the bedroom, leaving them for a few moments. She could hear them talking. The words they were using were absolutely crude and deplorable. She went back into the bathroom, distracted them and finished the bath.

After they were in bed, she thought about how and where they could possibly have heard such language. She knew that neither she nor Doug talked in that manner. She recalled that while they had been playing outside after supper, the single fellows had been changing a tire on one of the 4-wheel drive police vehicles. Gerri knew that the members had been prepared to go out on patrol, and had unexpectedly had to change the tire. The next day, she requested the fellows let her know when a tire needed changing. She would then have the children stay inside until the task was completed. Fortunately, she never heard those words from the children again.

Another incident Gerri remembers happened one Saturday evening before Mother's Day. At approximately 10:00 p.m. she answered the residence door. A man was standing there stating that he needed to talk to the police. While he was speaking, she noticed the pulse in his neck was really pounding. He explained that a child had been held by the grandfather in the front seat of the truck while the mother was in the back of the truck. The half-ton went over a bump, the passenger door flew open, and the child fell from the grandfather's lap out into the ditch. They stopped immediately, and when they got to the baby, it was dead. The man wanted to wait at the detachment until the police arrived.

By the time Gerri had radioed to the members out on patrol and returned to tell the man when the police would be back, she noticed that the pulse in her neck was also throbbing. Gerri found it difficult at times in a small detachment, to constantly live with these kinds of tragedies, but it also made her more appreciative of what she had.

On a nice summer day, a lady with one leg and using a crutch, had come to the detachment to talk to Doug. They happened to meet outside and stood there talking. The oldest Madill boy, about four at the time was playing outside. He spotted this lady, walked over to her and started to circle her, looking at her foot. He eventually bent over and looked up her skirt, Gerri assumed to find the missing leg. She viewed this from inside the house, while Doug was trying to keep a straight face when urging Lachie to go and play. Gerri concluded Doug must have been thinking of the joys of doing police work with the family underfoot.

The Madill dog attempted to get involved in the happenings at the detachment. She often chose to sleep on a portion of the detachment lawn so that she could be in the line of traffic to be petted by people. Sometimes she was a nuisance as well.

On one occasion, some men gave Doug and another member trouble while they were being arrested. The men were handcuffed together before being put into the police truck. Once they reached the detachment and the vehicle doors were opened, these men again attempted to fight with the members. A short-lived tussle ensued with the three prisoners and two policemen wrestling on the ground. The dog, that had been chewing on a big bone, took the bone in her mouth, walked over to the melee, and wagging her tail, dropped the bone as if asking to play as well. The fight ended quickly with only the dog being disappointed.

Late one Saturday night while Doug was out on patrol, Gerri received a phone call from the Hutterite Colony near the historical site of Fort Pitt. Their men had been digging, preparing the ground for the foundation of a new building. In the process, they had pushed up a skeleton. They stopped work, called and said they would like it checked out before Monday as they wanted to resume work. Gerri assumed that it was an "old" skeleton and did not radio the members. She left a note by the phone for Doug telling him to call the colony regarding a skeleton.

Gerri was asleep when Doug returned and he slept late the next day. When he came downstairs, he walked by the phone and saw the note. His immediate thought was that it might be a more recent skeleton. Gerri was informed that her "judgement call" had better be accurate. As it turned out, the skeleton was that of a sixteen-year-old aboriginal youth who had been in the ground for approximately one hundred years. There was a bullet hole through the skull. After that information, Gerri felt quite smug, stating that she knew how to screen calls. She went on to say that on occasion she figured the RCMP should have paid her, because her previous Social Work experience helped her manage calls and various crises that occurred.

One morning when Gerri knew she was alone at the Onion Lake Detachment, she heard some noise at the back door of the house. This startled her because nobody ever used that door (except the single fellows when they came to borrow food). When Gerri got to the door, she was even more startled. There was an elderly native man with long white braids wearing a rather dilapidated RCMP Stetson. She thought the Stetson was somehow connected to the man's visit.

Actually, he had come to lodge a complaint at the detachment, and as no members were present, of course, Gerri would do. He was an old bachelor who lived in his own small house. Members of the local Homemakers' Club had gone to give his house a spring-cleaning. He was most annoyed and did not want them in there again. He expected the police to keep them out. Gerri never did find out what the RCMP connection was and why he had the Stetson.

In small detachments, Gerri found she was often feeding many people, sometimes with prior warning and sometimes not. Usually, court date at Onion Lake involved feeding the judge and, or some lawyers. At Leader there were times during hunting season when she would feed breakfast to Game Officers.

On one occasion, at Onion Lake, Gerri was prepared to feed approximately ten extra people at noon. There were two dog men and others doing a search in the area. Gerri had two large meat loaves and many baked potatoes in the oven. Just as she was about to place the food on the table, a call came from North Battleford. Two suspects who had been involved in an armed robbery were spotted near St. Walburg to the east. The members were asked to provide assistance. At that point, all ten members left in a cavalcade of police vehicles.

They were all at Onion Lake to be fed the following day. The meat loaves were warmed up and the baked potatoes were made into a potato salad. This was before the days of microwave ovens.

On another occasion, the kitchen was being remodelled. The day the work started, Gerri managed to provide coffee for approximately thirty people throughout the day. At one point, the only place she had to sit was on a sawhorse.

Horses on the reserve could wander freely and would sometimes come to the Onion Lake Detachment to eat lawn grass. A few times, Gerri woke up at night and heard some rustling sounds outside. When she looked out, she could see these horses on the lawn and they were scratching themselves on the drain spout of the eaves troughs.

The horses tended to leave a "deposit". One morning when she looked out, she could see the horse droppings on the driveway and sidewalks. One horse had actually made a deposit directly in front of the detachment door. The single fellows were not too impressed when she woke them up to give them this information. Doug was away and the fellow that was second-in-charge had worked late into the night. He needed to clean up the mess before people started to come to the office. He asked that Gerri phone him the next time she heard the horses, as he would rather shoot than shovel.

While living in different small communities, Gerri found that each area had its own expectations of members' wives. One community was visibly disappointed when they found out that she taught piano lessons and not figure skating.

She recalls being asked to attend a social function in one community. When she offered to take along food, they told her to take whatever she wanted. In the previous community, she took a 9" x 13" cake with icing. She did the same in this community. When she gave the cake to the organizers of the event, they looked at it and said, "Is that all?" Later Gerri checked the table to see what others brought. The local tradition was to take a pan of squares that was 1.5 times the usual recipe (not single, not double). Her cake simply did not have enough calories, nor was it big enough. The adjacent community expected her to always bring pies. Gerri thought it would be a good idea if each member's wife left lists and recipes behind for the next wife.

People of some towns believed that if the policeman's wife did not have a large vegetable garden, she was quite lazy. The fact that one had outside employment did not count. It seemed that just when some of this treatment would become discouraging, there would be an occasion when somebody would show real appreciation for efforts the RCMP members and their wives put into the community.

The Madills eventually settled in Saskatoon where both Gerri and Doug participate in many community activities.

40

Some Northern Experiences

Sadie and Ken Conrad were transferred to the fly-in posting of Cumberland House in June of 1963. Sadie was six and a half months pregnant with their second child. They had placed all their possessions, except personal items in storage before flying off to the north and isolation. It was exciting and they loved it.

There was no doctor at Cumberland House. The detachment had neither telephone nor radio communication. Transportation was by bombardier for winter travel or boat for summer. On the positive side, the Conrads encountered some of the friendliest people they'd ever met, and they made fantastic friends.

Since Sadie had an Rh Negative factor with potential risk to the baby involved, the nurse at the Nursing Station was reluctant to have her deliver in Cumberland House. In September, Sadie and their two-year-old son flew to Manitoba where they stayed with her sister until the baby was born. On September 27th their daughter was born without any problems. In early October, Sadie and her children went back to Cumberland House. They arrived just in time for C.O. Perlson's "Tour of the North Inspection".

This officer was known for inspecting not only the offices and the men, but also the married residences. Because there was no phone or radio communication, there was no advance warning of his expected time of arrival. The first indication they had of someone arriving was when an aircraft flew low over the buildings. The drive from the airstrip to the detachment took only ten or fifteen minutes, not much time for any preparations. Everyone Sadie knew shuddered at the news of Perlson's imminent inspections, and a great deal of scrubbing, polishing and cleaning preceded his arrival. Although Sadie had a toddler and a newborn, she felt she must do a thorough house cleaning. She was greatly relieved when the man didn't express any fault with their residence.

Whenever time was drawing near for another inspection, Sadie made sure her housework was up to date. Every morning before the dreaded inspection took place, Sadie asked their two-year-old to take only a few toys out of his toy box. Being an obedient little fellow, he did as he was asked. The day after the inspection, the child sat beside his toy box awaiting the routine instruction. When none came, he finally asked if he could play.

Sadie said, "Sure, with all the toys." Sadie related that in one motion he tipped the box, and toys went flying over the living room. She joined him on the floor. "We played instead of preparing for some C.O. to come in with his white gloves to check on my housekeeping," Sadie said. "I was annoyed at the invasion at the time, and now I'm outraged that we allowed ourselves to be that manipulated. I've often thought I would liked to have given Perlson a piece of my mind, but given the opportunity, I would have bowed and called him 'Sir'."

The Conrads' next posting was in Lac La Ronge. Sadie recalls that socializing was an important part of northern detachment life. Most of it was informal and impromptu, but when the event of the year came along, northerners pulled out all the stops. Such an event was the Firemen's Ball held in the largest available hall in Lac La Ronge. The hall, little more than a shell of a building, was made festive with candle light and elaborate decorations which helped to hide at least a few of its faults.

"It was spectacular, or so we thought," Sadie said. Many weeks of planning and preparation proceeded the event. Dress was no less than formal, and anyone who knew how to operate a sewing machine, and some who didn't, would set about the task of creating a gown for the occasion. Since most wives had young children, the sewing was done mainly in the late evenings. When children were in bed, their mothers concentrated on the task at hand without interruption. Many a midnight heard the whine of the old Singer.

Baby-sitters were booked for the evening and there was usually a pre-ball cocktail party to attend. At any rate, the ball was quite the event and was awaited with much anticipation. The evening arrived and the Conrads had a great time.

Dancing was in full swing and probably three-quarters into the evening when Ken was called to the phone. Sadie thought nothing of that since, when they were out, he was often called to, or about, work. This time Ken returned to tell her they had to go home immediately. She got on her coat and winter boots, and carrying her high heels she followed Ken out. On the way home he explained that an intoxicated native had entered their house. At that time doors were never locked. He was terrorizing the baby-sitter. Sadie thought that was bad enough, but she worried about what might be happening to her babies.

The car had scarcely stopped when she was running toward the house. The intruder chose just then to go outside and Sadie let into him with her high heels. Fortunately for him, one of the constables on duty arrived and intervened. The native, with great relief at seeing the constable begged, "Mountie, get me away from this crazy woman." He docilely accompanied the policeman into the cellblock. The baby-sitter was calmed down and the children were groggy and confused but no harm was done.

Lac La Ronge has some of the greatest tourism opportunities in Northern Saskatchewan. Tourism began there in the late 1930's with fishing. It was the site of early fur trading. Pictographs painted on granite rock with natural ochre colour show hunting scenes. In 1906 All Saints Anglican Church was built.

41

Adventures Beginning in 1947

Dorothy remembers what occurred on her husband's twenty-sixth birthday. It was March 29, 1947 when Ewen applied for permission to marry her. He had been refused the previous September because he was only twenty-five. He was sent to Pierceland to do forestry patrol, but was promised leave if his request was granted. Because Dorothy's mother was slated for surgery, they set the date for May 3 so her mother could have the operation after the wedding. On Thursday, May 1st, Dorothy got a letter from Ewen saying permission to marry was approved, but his leave was cancelled. Everything was ready for the wedding, so Dorothy and her mother were in a state.

Her dad went to see Prince Albert's Officer Commanding who was very sympathetic. He got in touch with the O.C. in North Battleford, and three days leave was granted. There was a problem informing Ewen, since there were no telephones in Pierceland, neither did the RCMP have a two-way radio there, and the roads were not always passable. Fortunately, Ewen had caught a ride in a truck over to Loon Lake to phone Dorothy. She told him the news about his leave. There happened to be a patrol going through the area from Meadow Lake, and Ewen was able to travel out with it. Everything worked out as planned.

After their three-day honeymoon, they were en route to Pierceland. Constable Anderson at Loon Lake was to have reserved a hotel room for them, but there was none available. A friend who was staying with him was sleeping on the studio lounge. The friend slept in the cells that night. The constable slept in his own single bed, and the newlyweds had the studio lounge in the tiny quarters. There was a chemical toilet and no running water, and certainly no privacy for a newly married couple. Constable Anderson took them to Goodsoil the next day and the policeman stationed there drove them to Pierceland.

Dorothy and Ewen spent the first six weeks of their marriage in the hotel at Pierceland. There was no extra charge for Dorothy sharing Ewen's room. He was on an expense account, and his pay cheque for the month of May left him with only $36.00. He paid for Dorothy's board out of this. Because Tuesday and Friday were meatless days in the dining room, the menu was herrings, eggs or sardines. The Grays were usually invited out on those days, as everyone knew what the menu would be.

Wilkie was the Grays' next posting where they lived in an apartment above the post office and next to the RCMP office. The town fire siren was right above the living room. It blew every noon hour, as well as whenever there was a fire in the town. The siren initially frightened the Grays' two small children, but its noise soon became a time for them to run about laughing while holding their hands over their ears. In time, night sirens barely disturbed their sleep. There were other disturbances for their parents.

One night at Wilkie, Dorothy and Ewen had just gone to bed when people at the door awakened them. Ewen grabbed his trousers and a shirt and took off to a terrible accident. When helping the ambulance attendants pick up the seriously injured, he split his trousers. At the Hospital, one of the nurses gave him a bunch of safety pins to hold the seam together. As there was one person killed, he was busy all day with the investigation, and he had no time to change his pants. The person killed, and others in the accident, were all nice Wilkie teenagers, and the community was in shock. It was a difficult case for Ewen to deal with.

Besides supporting stunned and grieving parents, Ewen had not slept for forty hours. The doctor, knowing Ewen was upset and overtired, came to the office that evening to give him a sleeping pill. He was instructed to get into a hot tub, and then take the pill before going to bed. Ewen got the instructions confused and took the pill before getting into the tub. Dorothy had a dreadful time getting his six foot, two inch, two hundred and twenty-pound frame out of the tub and into bed. He slept for twelve hours without even turning over.

Wilkie is a town of about 1400 and is located southwest of Battleford. The first RNWMP detachment was established there in 1908. In 1914 the Wilkie Press published a letter from Mrs. F. Howard, wife of Major D. M. Howard. The letter travelled from a northern Manitoba detachment in Port Nelson to the wife of a Wilkie lawyer. The letter reads:

> *My dear Mrs. Laycock: Your postcard sent to me at Halifax reached me a short time ago. We are just now expecting our winter patrol with letters; we will be so glad to get news. We have such a hard time of it – we had not sufficient supplies, some mistake was made either in Regina or Ottawa and a requisition for an officer and three men, instead; one officer and seven men came in and we had not enough coal. Then*

this year, deer, birds, fish, are all scarce and there has been a disease amongst the dogs so we have had one of the hardest years one could have.

We are faring a little better just now but the lack of fresh food is terrible. Our houses are like B.C. houses and doors and windows are badly broken and don't fit, so we can't live in them. The floors don't join and there are large holes you can put your hand through, they are like large barns with no ceilings. We had no tarpaper; no lumber so could not make them warm. We got some beaverboard, just enough to put in a ceiling in one room and line the walls a little; with this we had to be content for we could do no more. January was our coldest month and the temperature kept from 35 to 48 below and for three weeks we had from 50 to 64 below at night – it was terrible; I have had to keep to my bed all the time from New Year's Day till now; even now I do not get up till 11 a.m. and am allowed to go out only in the middle of the day. I was seized one morning with chill and rheumatic neuralgia set in – I have suffered dreadfully. At first we thought it was a stroke, it came on instantaneously while I was doing my hair – it affected the whole of my right side and I was afraid of my life for a while. Sometimes I think I won't ever come out, I shall be leaving my bones here – we have had such a rough deal; we have no furniture; I have sat on a wooden box and shall have to until supplies come in next August.

I wonder if they will make the same mistake again? If so we should certainly freeze to death or starve – it seems terrible that people can be so careless when things are to come to a country like this, where you can't get anything and depend entirely on them to send things in.

I hope you are all well; our united regards to Mr. Laycock.

Yours sincerely, F. Howard.

(After reading about these deplorable conditions, it is easy to minimize lesser problems we experienced on detachments. Our trying situations, however, seemed real enough to us when compared to the life we had left, in order to join our husbands at their postings.)

The Grays moved to Onion Lake in 1952 where there was neither electricity, nor running water. The bedrooms were finished with cardboard boxes nailed to the studs and calcimined. They had, what seemed like, a mile of stovepipe that they had to clean every six weeks because of the green wood they burned in the pot-bellied stove. The

Grays learned that burning green wood would create a build-up of creosote in the pipes, which could spontaneously ignite, causing a difficult blaze to extinguish.

Their quarters were so small that they were forced to put their chemical toilet in the cell. It would otherwise have been in a bedroom or the living room. Fortunately, there weren't many prisoners. When the cells were in use, Ewen had to remove the toilet to the outside facility.

They had a lovely garden at Onion Lake, but cattle from the Indian reserve got in one night, tramping over and eating the whole thing. Dorothy was angry as she thought of the work she had put into the garden. The gate was not very substantial, but Ewen repaired it as best he could.

One day a woman called the detachment to speak to Dorothy. Since her caller's common-law husband was in the cells, she wanted Dorothy to look after her horses. The policeman had arrested her husband so she reasoned Dorothy should help her out.

On another occasion when there was a woman in the cells, her elderly husband phoned to ask Dorothy who was going to look after him. Again, the inference was that since the policeman had inconvenienced him, she should be willing to help out.

Twins were born to the Grays while they were at Onion Lake. Dorothy went into labour in October, a month early and about ten at night. Ewen called Blower's Store, and the owner's son went out to the Indian Department Hospital to pick up the nurse and take her to the detachment. She examined Dorothy and said they'd never make it to Lloydminster, so she prepared for the delivery.

She gathered newspapers, towels and a spool of white thread to tie the cord. Dorothy and Ewen were quite concerned about having a home delivery. By 4:30 in the morning the nurse decided all was not well, and she called the doctor. He said he had no idea how to get to the detachment at Onion Lake so he told her to take the expectant mother into Lloydminster. Ewen got the neighbours to come and stay with their two little girls and they started out for town. The nurse accompanied them.

To get to the Meridian Ferry, they had to follow a rough country road. There was a delay at the river while Ewen roused the ferry operator from bed. The men had trouble starting the ferry's engine, but they eventually got it functioning. It was a terrible trip for Dorothy. Her labour pains were magnified with each bump in the road and with the delays encountered. She was in such agony, she remembers wishing she would die. They finally arrived at Lloydminster. At the hospital she was given a shot in her hip, and she didn't know anything until the afternoon when she was told they had twins. She hadn't known she had been carrying twins so their birth was a big surprise to both Ewen and Dorothy.

Ewen had returned to Onion Lake before the twins arrived as the Indian Department nurse was anxious to get back to her patients, and Ewen had two children at home who needed him. Before going to see his new son and daughter, Ewen had to clean out the back seat of the police car. Once he had removed the blood-soaked papers and pads, and had washed the back seat, he walked around the vehicle to see if it needed polishing. Through the back window of the police car he saw a big box against the glass. The large letters on the box spelled out the words SANITARY NAPKINS. He quickly retrieved it and put it away before driving back to the city.

The next move took the Gray family to Esterhazy in December of 1954. Their belongings were transported in the old RCMP truck and they did their own packing and loading. All Dorothy's preserves of fruit, vegetables and meat, about 350 quarts, were frozen in the week it took to move. The delay took place because of mechanical problems with the truck. Dorothy was furious when she thought of all the work and expense involved in preserving the food. There was no insurance to help replace the food, so it was a hardship for the family having to buy everything they needed. Dorothy was grateful for professional movers after that transfer, but she seldom preserved food again.

The Esterhazy house was huge. It had started as three granaries and had been added to until there were about thirteen rooms. The gravel highway ran past the detachment, and dust flew every time a car passed. Dorothy could clean one day, and the children's footprints would show in the dust the next day.

Ewen shovelled twenty-two tons of coal into the stoker in the winter, and it seemed more came out in clinkers. Also, there was no door on the coal bin, so the house filled with dust each time coal was delivered. The Grays could hear mice running around at night, and they caught many in traps, but could only put traps where the children couldn't get at them. The basement of that house had about a foot of water in it all one summer because of heavy rainfall. It came in as fast as it could be pumped out, so it was just left.

While posted in Esterhazy, Dorothy urged Ewen to take a civilian with him to drive on two occasions. The first time, there had been an armed robbery, and he was ordered to check all cars at a highway intersection. He took the fellow who did night guard duty for him; he was to stay in the car, but if Ewen didn't come back immediately, he was to go for help. As it happened, there were no suspects on the highway that night.

The next time, Ewen had his arm in a cast, and was supposed to be off duty. He had been involved in a fight with a drunk while trying to arrest him and the result was a broken arm. When he got a call about people breaking into a Credit Union seventeen miles away, the other policeman was out on patrol with the cruiser. Dorothy called a friend who drove the Gray's private car for Ewen, and they caught the people in the act. In fact, they solved another break in at the same time.

Esterhazy, in southeast Saskatchewan, was named after Hungarian Count Paul Oscar Esterhazy who founded the community in 1902. It has been known for its major potash industry since 1957. Population is 2,827.

After living in such inconvenient places, the family loved the little house they bought in Yorkton. It was also a pleasure later to live in the new detachment building in Punnichy. There was, however, one drawback in Punnichy. The septic tank was buried in the middle of the front lawn, and several times when Dorothy had ladies for tea, the tank had to be pumped out. There was an unpleasant odour at such times. In the winter, Old John, the septic tank cleaner, used to put the hose to his mouth and blow on it to thaw it out. Dorothy found she had to adjust to situations foreign to her.

She was hired as the matron to accompany a female mental patient to the psychiatric hospital in North Battleford. While Ewen completed the necessary forms for the patient's transfer, and tended to other office matters, Dorothy kept the woman with her. The woman was so psychotic she wouldn't let Dorothy out of her sight, following her everywhere, even to the bathroom.

Often when the Grays had company, Dorothy had to excuse herself while she went to search a drunken female prisoner. It was very difficult to hire anyone to do matron duty; it was much more convenient for Ewen to have his wife do the job.

The family next moved to an upstairs apartment over the detachment office in Tisdale. The apartment was small, but they managed. Dorothy had to go through her husband's office to get to the laundry in the basement. This proved to be most inconvenient at times.

In Tisdale there was a cafe from which to order prisoner meals, and there was a matron to search and guard female prisoners. Because of this, Dorothy was able to fully concentrate on caring for her family.

Widowed, she now resides in Saskatoon where she keeps active and has a wide circle of friends.

42

Cultural Awareness

"While posted on an isolated reserve in Pelican Narrows, I was constantly reminded of cultural differences," said Betty Knechtel of her experiences during the mid-seventies. She had grown up in Halifax, Nova Scotia and knew nothing of life in the small northern Saskatchewan village where she had gone to teach.

Her first purchase in Pelican Narrows was a pair of rubber boots from the Hudson's Bay Company, the one and only store. There was no pavement; mud was everywhere. Another day, Betty went to the Bay looking for suntan lotion. The workers had never heard of it, and in broken English asked what it was. When Betty explained it was a lotion to help make her skin darker, they giggled and said,

"What do you want that for? You're nice and white already." She shrugged her shoulders and made an exit. The natives were often puzzled by Betty's actions and they gave her cause to question herself. She had attempted to grow a patch of lawn beside her trailer, and one day when she was trimming the grass, a group of natives strolled by.

"Why are you growing grass just so you can cut if off?" one asked.

"That's really stupid," commented another. Betty thought to herself, I guess they're right.

Once again, Betty came up against native logic when a few of them watched her jogging. "Hey, white girl, why are you running when no one is chasing you?" She discovered the locals were watching out for her in a unique way.

"I was always fascinated by the Northern Lights," Betty said. "I'd never seen them before. They would dance rhythmically and flash brilliant colours across the sky." Every evening when the lights appeared, Betty would stand outside, gazing in wonder and sometimes tried to capture the sight on film. The natives often yelled at her to get inside or run and hide. After several episodes of hearing their pleas, she asked for an explanation.

"The lights are gods, and when they dance and come close to earth, they will capture you and take you up to heaven," they told her. When Betty realized how superstitious her neighbours were, she became more cautious not to upset them.

Betty looked forward to report card time and interviews with parents. The children spoke only Cree until they learned English in school. Their parents spoke mostly Cree as well. Tradition in Pelican Narrows had each teacher go from house to house, with an interpreter, to meet the families.

Betty eagerly went by snowmobile, with the interpreter to show the way and to translate. Most families displayed little or no interest in what she said. Survival by trapping, hunting and fishing was their main concern at that time. Betty soon realized the people were also intimidated by her presence. The interviews were reduced to a brief introduction, a smile and a few positive comments about each child. Betty noticed most people smiled back, but kept their distance.

One home stands out in Betty's memory. The woman of the house was cooking pancakes on the wood stove, not in a frying pan, but directly on the stovetop. That was surprising enough for Betty, but beside the pancakes reposed a beaver, belly-up with a butcher knife sticking out of its middle. The sight was rather unsettling for Betty.

The native children often came to visit in her trailer. Compared to shacks or tents some of them lived in, the trailer was full of wonders. Betty loved to watch the children's faces as they experienced a new world just yards from their own homes. The flushing toilet and hot water from a tap fascinated them. Colour television, the dishwasher, and electric appliances of all kinds seemed to be such wonders. They expressed disbelief at the use of an electric can opener.

"Are you too lazy to do it yourself?" inquired one small soul. Ever since Betty's Pelican Narrows experiences she often questions how and why she does certain things.

Betty married Scott Knechtel, an RCMP constable stationed at Pelican Narrows. They returned to the village from their honeymoon in July, 1977. At that time there were no telephones or paved roads in the village, and the only electricity came from a small community generator. Nurses at the nurses' station provided medical care. In times of emergencies, many locals also relied on an RCMP officer or a teacher.

Scott was working on the evening of their return to the north. Betty was excited to be in their trailer unpacking wedding gifts. She was sharing the fun with Val, the young nurse who was in charge of the Nurses' Station while the two experienced nurses were on days off. Val was just out of nursing school; northern experiences were new to her. While the two young women chatted and while Betty unwrapped wedding gifts, the trailer door opened. A native woman was stooped over, holding her abdomen.

"Come quick," she yelled. "The baby's here."

"I guess you'll have to hurry and get her to the nursing station," Betty said. "I can't help because I fainted during the child birth film I saw at a First Aid Course." Val's easy going personality suddenly changed.

She said, "What do I do? What do I do? I've never delivered a baby before. Betty, you have to help me." Betty stared at her friend for a moment when she realized she was serious. Betty took a deep breath, silently asked for strength and went to the woman's aid.

"We stumbled over rocks and tree stumps as we struggled to take the woman to the nurses' station." Betty helped the woman onto the examination table.

Val said, "Oh, my God, oh, my God. Betty, make sure to catch the baby."

Since this was Betty's first time to witness a live birth, she didn't know what to expect. There was no time for hand washing or for putting on gloves, but Betty thought she had better look to see if the woman's water had broken. What she saw was the baby's head emerging. The baby was born very fast, needing little assistance. "You have a baby girl," Betty announced to the mother.

"Oh, no. I have four of them at home already," came the reply. "What's your name?"

"Betty."

"That's what I'll call her, Betty," she mumbled in a monotone.

Once the infant was born, Val seemed to regain some composure. She instructed Betty to wash the baby's eyes with special eye drops, to cut the cord and wrap the baby in a sheet.

"What are you going to do?" Betty inquired. Val explained she needed to prepare for delivery of the afterbirth. Betty remained puzzled.

The nearest hospital was Flin Flon, Manitoba where the nurse arranged to have patient and baby flown. Within two hours of the woman's arrival at Betty's door, she was boarding the ski plane, baby in one arm and afterbirth in a plastic grocery bag, draped over the other arm.

"To this day, I'm very thankful I never had a baby at the nursing station," Betty said in conclusion.

Moving day ...

43

The Ups and Downs in Lumsden

Ellen and Dennis Parsons have fond memories of their seven years in Lumsden, even though their introduction was disappointing. When they moved there in the spring of 1962, Dennis opened the one-man detachment, which did not as yet have radio contact. Ellen, with tongue in cheek, describes the accommodation for living quarters and office space as "interesting".

The shabby house had been built in 1903 and was situated on two lots, one for the large house and its circular drive, and another for a flower garden surrounded by trees. The grounds were heavily overgrown, and although it was obvious the house had once been a grand and gracious home, it was sadly in need of attention.

Ellen commented, "I personally feel homework had not been done in the selection of an appropriate building." The home had been vacant for quite some time, and it had received no care since the owners had moved to British Columbia.

When the Parsons arrived at the detachment just after the moving van, they were full of excitement to begin this new phase of their life. Leaving their suitcases on the sidewalk, they hurried in to view this majestic, old place which was to be their new home and work site. It was a disappointment to discover no cleaning had been done, dirt and dust being everywhere. The attic space of the two-storied home had been converted into a finished room, but was full of bats. Ellen and Dennis made a quick exit. Dennis took his wife and little boy to a Regina hotel where they planned to stay while exterminators did their work. Upon arrival at the hotel, it was discovered they were without luggage. The Parsons had been so shocked and disappointed, and in their hurried retreat had given no thought to their luggage. Dennis drove back to retrieve it. By the time he again arrived in Regina, he had made four trips, having started the day in Melfort.

Within a few days, the Parsons were getting settled in their Lumsden home. The basement had a dirt floor. The owners had owned two large dogs, and it was only too obvious, they had used the basement to deposit their droppings. Ellen and Dennis made many trips up the stairs carrying tubs of dog excrement. Their neighbours, who owned a farm, provided sheep dip. The Parsons used the dip to saturate the basement floor in an attempt to disinfect it and to give it a fresher scent. The neighbour was also kind enough to provide his truck so the foul earth could be removed from the property.

After cleaning the house and settling in, Ellen and Dennis tackled the yard work in an attempt at improving the appearance of the detachment grounds. One day while they were busily employed outdoors, Ellen in shorts and Dennis in fatigues, a visitor arrived from Regina Subdivision Office. To the Parsons, the visit had seemed genuinely friendly, but two days later, a memo arrived. It would seem the visitor was of the opinion Dennis and Ellen were improperly dressed during office hours.

Another memorable time concerned one of the first night patrols Dennis undertook while at Lumsden. When Ellen awoke to daybreak and discovered her husband had not returned, she became worried. Since the detachment did not as yet have radio contact, Ellen could do nothing but wait. Dennis eventually returned on foot after his vehicle became stuck somewhere in the valley. He wore breeches and heavy, high boots, the order of the day, and as result had a number of blisters on his feet. Ellen was only too glad to see him return, blisters and all.

Ellen was pleased to have running water, but because it was not suitable for drinking, it was necessary to carry water from a well at the end of the block. As inconvenient as this was, it provided a social outlet, since people visited when meeting at the well.

Another inconvenience was the sewage system. The only bathroom was on the second floor of the large building and included a rather unique flushing system. Whenever the toilet was flushed, its user had to run down two flights of stairs to kick a motor in order for it to operate drainage to the septic tank. At one point, the tank had to be dug up and repaired.

Ellen washed clothes every second day since her son, only a year old, wore diapers. The wringer washer was in the basement and the clothes were dried on an outside line necessitating many trips up and downstairs. One day as Ellen was putting laundry through the wringer, the furnace clicked in and she was shocked to see flames licking through furnace pipes beneath the overhead flooring. It was subsequently discovered the pipes were quite worn out and could have caused a house fire at any time. Ellen considered it a miracle one had not occurred. As she said, "This was the last straw. We felt unsafe until the Force gave us the go ahead to seek out more suitable living quarters and office space."

The Parsons moved to a much newer but smaller home, a bungalow with no basement, only a crawl space. The carport was made into an office. The back exit now led from the kitchen into the office. Ellen tried to time her entrance or exit when there was no one in the office; otherwise she used the front door. The Parsons' second son was born soon after the move into these quarters. As the boys grew, Ellen found it difficult to keep them from visiting their dad in the office.

One evening while Dennis was doing paper work, he kept hearing odd noises. He checked outside a couple of times, but there was nothing to be seen. When scratching sounds persisted, he opened the door to the crawl space. He encountered a large rat nestled in some curled-up garden hose. Dennis, carrying his large, issue flashlight, flung it at the lowly creature. His aim was accurate, the blow stunning the rat, enabling him to dispose of it. After searching to discover how this unwelcome visitor had gained access, Dennis found and repaired a small opening. That resolved the rat problem.

Ellen was soon to discover how accurate her aim was. While chopping vegetables in preparation for the evening meal, she caught sight of a mouse scampering across the kitchen floor. Without thinking she flung the utility knife in the mouse's direction. Much to her surprise and to her husband's, Ellen made a bull's eye hit, breaking the mouse's spine.

This second detachment building was located just off the old highway, its driveway backing onto it. Directly across from them was a service station, which was closed every night. Some people travelling Highway #11 seemed to think the detachment could accommodate their gas needs during night hours.

On one occasion, during the middle of the night, the Parsons awoke to non-stop ringing of the doorbell. When Dennis answered the office door he was met by some young people demanding he call the service station operator to come to their assistance. When they were told the operator never came out at night, the stubborn youths remained in the detachment driveway drinking beer while they waited for gas in the morning. Ellen had left washing out on her umbrella clothesline only to discover the night people had amused themselves by strewing her clothes everywhere.

Ellen spent many hours answering the two-way radio once it was installed. Like all wives of small detachments, she was able to help her husband in a variety of ways. Usually falling to the wives was the boring and time-consuming job of filing Index Cards, which included photos and data of wanted or released convicts. One time when Ellen and their little boy accompanied Dennis to Regina, they remained in the car while Dennis was in Regina Town Station. This undesirable street had a number of young men lounging against walls. Some of the men seemed intent on getting Ellen's attention. She attempted to look inconspicuous, but found this difficult since she was almost nine months pregnant.

When Dennis returned to the car, she told him, "Those fellows look familiar, especially one of them, but I don't know why." She indicated the one she referred to.

After glancing at the loiterers Dennis replied, "Well, I'd say you recognize him since you recently filed his Index Card." Ellen was surprised, not expecting to encounter one of "her" convicts on a city street.

The Parsons family made their third and last move in Lumsden to newly built detachment quarters. They had the privilege of living in it for two years and found it a wonderful change from their two previous, inconvenient homes.

Because they were located on the river's edge, they installed a chain link fence to provide some protection for the children. During the town's 1969 flooding, their place was sandbagged up to the doors. Ellen and the children were invited to stay in Regina for two weeks with the family of a bank manager she had formerly worked for. After the water receded, she was relieved there had been no damage to their personal property, but she was sorry for many others in the community who were less fortunate.

After living in Lumsden for seven years, Ellen felt very much at home. Shortly after they were transferred away, Ellen and Dennis returned for a wedding. While in the community hall enjoying seeing all the familiar faces, they were asked how they felt about having moved on. Ellen broke into tears and replied, "We'd come back in a minute."

The gentleman asking the question said, "What did you expect? You young people grew up here with us." They certainly had grown up, their many experiences having ensured that. Lumsden and its citizens will always remain in the hearts of the Parsons.

44

Snakes and Other Surprises

Phyllis Stephens had always listened with admiration to the exciting stories that other RCMP wives told about living on one-man or two-man detachments. They seemed to appeal to her "Mrs. Mike" romanticism. The stories were always told with a sense of humour, and they described wonderful and innovative coping skills. So, when the Stephens were posted to Bengough in 1973, Phyllis was quite excited!

She found the Bengough area to be a fascinating place; it was a mass of purple crocuses in spring, cactus in summer, although desolate in winter. She learned the area was also rich with tales and traces of Northwest Territories history.

The living quarters were very comfortable. Phyllis was relieved there was no outdoor toilet or indoor "pail" she had heard about. There were three bedrooms, and the cement floor of the basement was painted. The fact that the pink bathroom fixtures were brown-stained from iron was acceptable as everyone in town had that problem. It was difficult when the town regularly flushed the water mains, which made the water really brown. Anything white never stayed white – yellow at best – at worst, there were really brown iron stains. That included everyone's underwear and dishcloths, but no worry, if Phyllis soaked them in undiluted toilet cleaner they came out fairly clean. This was hard on the hands, but it was necessary. The iron stains hardly showed on the khaki uniform shirts.

Drinking water was hauled from a spring-fed well on a nearby farm. The water was stored in a large, blue plastic camping container, which had a place of honour on the kitchen counter. The children knew all about water conservation, and it was never wasted in the home. One day when the neighbour's five-year-old daughter drained the Stephens' drinking water, Phyllis chastised her. Two days later, Phyllis was sorry to learn the child was diagnosed with acute diabetes, which explained her unnatural thirst.

The water supply system in Bengough was unreliable, and had a habit of frequently breaking down. The water tower actually collapsed after the Stephens family left.

Detachment inspections were a highlight of their life. They were not favourite times, but memorable none-the-less. There was much tension and commotion. The whole family was put on alert – even the dog. Neighbours were warned to stay clear. Phyllis had been quite sick and couldn't do the many linoleum floors. Appearances were very important, so her husband, Ed, as Corporal in charge, vacuumed, scrubbed and waxed all the floors. He and the Constable, sweat dripping off their brows, cleaned and dusted every room in the barracks including the cells and the garage.

The lawn had to be cut, the cars vacuumed, scrubbed and polished. In all the haste one of the Constables backed the patrol car over Phyllis's vacuum. There was much "spit and polish", scrubbing and ironing until boots, uniforms, windows and furniture were in top condition. Reams of paper work had to be in order, in both French and English.

"Crack in th' floor my fanny — that thing just MOVED!!!"

Last, but not least, meals had to be planned and prepared because there wasn't anywhere else for the "brass" to eat in town. Cooking for the prisoners didn't bother Phyllis, cooking for the Staff Sergeant was "so-so", but preparing meals for the Brass was nerve-racking. Phyllis thought that if she had a culinary failure, promotions would not be forthcoming.

Court days were another traumatic experience. There was great commotion. It was best if the wife and children were out of sight and out of mind. The members were long on hours and short on temper.

During "usual" times, the hours worked were long, involving most weekends and there were middle of the night or mid-meal calls back to duty. Family life was limited to holidays, lunch and supper breaks and occasional weekends off. That's the way it was – expected and accepted.

The family did enjoy some picnics in the Big Muddy Valley, up on a hillside by the old North West Mounted Police cemetery. They found fresh water springs, ancient leaf fossils and felt the ghosts of the pioneers and native peoples on the hills and among the tepee rings and buffalo jumps.

There were snakes including rattlers, although, if people stepped carefully, they weren't a problem, or so Phyllis was told. She had a phobia for snakes, harmless or otherwise. She knew there were crickets and baby frogs in the basement, but nothing was done about them. The rent was right and she didn't complain enough.

One day Phyllis went down to the basement to take clothes out of the dryer. She was barefoot as it was very hot and there was no air conditioning. As she walked toward the dryer, a garter snake slithered out from under the dryer. If she'd fallen off a cliff she couldn't have been more shocked. She panicked! She leapt straight in the air, and didn't remember landing until she hit the stairs on the dead run.

Panting and panic-stricken, she ran into the office attached to the living quarters, only to find the men were out. She tried radioing the patrol car, however because the calls had to go through Regina, she wasn't getting a response. She ran outside, but none of the neighbours were home. Back in the quarters, she phoned the Constable's wife who worked at the bank. Irrational? Crazy? Of course, but this was panic time! The house had been taken over by her worst fear – snakes! The Constable's wife told the bank manager, who lived across the street from the barracks, and he, thinking she was being robbed, jumped in his car and went tearing over to rescue her.

She was soon the laughing stock of Bengough. Snakes were everywhere – part of Bengough and life in the Big Muddy. Neighbours told her stories of snakes coming out of the phone, kitchen cupboard, ceilings, and hanging from the walls of raised houses. But this was her house! The next day she came home from work at the hospital to find her husband and the owner of the barracks, calmly sitting in the office next to the basement stairs. These two men informed her they couldn't find any snakes, and they thought she had probably seen cracks in the basement floor. She turned the corner, looked down the stairs and said,

"If it's just cracks, the cracks are moving." Curling up at the bottom of the stairs was a snake. "The" snake? It was hard to say. The men found five including a dead one in the bottom of the dryer where she'd been reaching in for the clothes. The entry hole through the crawl space under the barracks was eventually sealed, but only after Phyllis refused to do the wash. Finally the snakes were eliminated from her life.

Her mother had told her stories of her childhood on the homestead. She described how, one particular fall season, snakes fell out of the blanket cupboard and curled up on the beds. So, Phyllis dreamed of snakes in her bed and closets for years. It was a bit disconcerting for her husband whenever she screeched and flung off the blankets in the middle of the night. The adrenaline starts to flow whenever she tells her own snake stories.

Bengough is called the Gateway to the Big Muddy, as it is located on the edge of the Big Muddy Valley north of the Montana/Saskatchewan border. The Big Muddy Valley is an ancient watercourse formed during the last glacial period.

Assiniboia, Blackfeet, the Bloods, and the Sarsis Indians once occupied the open prairie. Henry Kelsey, a Hudson's Bay Company employee, was the first white man to see the open prairies. The Big Muddy Badlands were once a home to outlaws that came north from the United States.

The town derived its name from John Wilson Bengough, one of Canada's prolific and brilliant cartoonists. The village was incorporated in 1911 and its present population is 500. The RCMP detachment has two members.

45

Remembering Spiritwood

Verna and Jim Telford with their two babies lived above Lloydminster's post office in 1953 and 1954. Verna remembers a lot of oil trucks driving by on the streets below, and dust rising in gigantic clouds. Their residence was hot and stuffy with storm windows remaining in place all year. Summer's only breath of fresh air came when Verna opened the north-facing fire escape door. Noise was an ever-present fact in the suite. Bags of mail were loaded and unloaded each day, starting about 4:30 a.m. Accompanying the truck motor and slamming doors were the driver's loud songs. If all that wasn't enough to ensure broken sleep, the nearby Royal Cafe provided more disturbances. After they completed their shifts in the restaurant, young, male Chinese immigrants returned to their upstairs rooms where they endlessly played Chinese records. When the Telfords were transferred to their first small detachment, Verna viewed it as an escape.

Their children were five months and eighteen months when the family moved to Spiritwood in January of 1955. Verna was relieved to be in a nice home even though she had to draw drinking water from a well across the street. Having been raised on a Saskatchewan farm, she was no stranger to the pail and rope routine. Because the office was located in the basement, Verna often found people wandering into her kitchen when they took the wrong door at the head of the stairs.

Unique to Spiritwood was private ownership of the electrical power. Verna soon learned not to wash clothes on Monday as most of the town was doing so. The cesspool had a habit of cracking on occasion, at which time a man who operated a trenching business was summoned for repairs. The same man, a likeable person, assisted Jim in transporting prisoners. He and his wife spent many hours playing cards and visiting with the Telfords, becoming their closest friends.

Verna, being an ardent curler, had a wonderful time curling; the rink was only half a block away. She was fortunate a neighbour lady loved to baby-sit her children. When they were a little older, she spent many a pleasant hour teaching them to skate on the open-air rink across the alley.

Verna enjoyed the "Hobo" teas in Spiritwood. She recalls having fourteen ladies descend on her one afternoon. She'd had a premonition they were coming, and had lots of baking on hand for the occasion.

Verna also became friends with a number of people from a nearby Hungarian settlement, meeting them when they were on their way to the RCMP office. When an old chap from the settlement had to appear in court in the basement office, he brought Verna two chickens in a gunnysack. These chickens, still in their sack, hopped around the office while court was in session. After court, Verna and the children went downstairs to view the situation. The children were quite amused to see the sack jumping around. The magistrate was rather amused as well, but he found the chicken owner guilty of making home brew and was levied a fine. Verna suspected the old fellow had hoped he might have an easier time in court since he'd arrived bearing gifts. That evening, the Telfords made a hasty trip to a farm to give the chickens away.

Another family from the settlement brought Verna a huge, oven-ready goose after she had assisted them when Jim was away from the detachment. A woman appeared at the door one lovely fall day about noon and announced that her brother-in-law had hung himself in the oat bin. She reported that family members had cut him down and they felt he was still alive.

Because Verna knew the town's physician was away with her husband, she offered to phone the hospital matron. Verna and the matron decided that even though the chap was likely dead, the matron would have the janitor drive her out to the family's farm with a tank of oxygen. They wanted the family to have a sense of being helped. The next day, Jim took the body to North Battleford in the police car. Shortly after this incident, the gift of a goose appeared.

Verna recalls opening the refrigerator one morning and discovering human organs bottled in alcohol. The previous night she had heard Jim opening and closing the refrigerator when he'd come home late after attending an autopsy. She had thought he was likely getting himself a snack, but upon coming across the human remains, she realized he would be taking them to the North Battleford pathologist that day.

"It's a small world" are the words that came to Verna's mind after she experienced the following incident. Jim had picked up a mental patient that he was preparing to transport to North Battleford. The fellow was very stubborn, saying he wasn't going anywhere until he had a cup of coffee. Jim took him into the kitchen and asked Verna to make coffee while he phoned for escort assistance. Verna noticed the man watched her every move when finally he said, "I know you".

"Oh, I'm sure you have me mixed up with someone else," she said. The patient proceeded to tell her he remembered she had been a telephone operator at Rouleau, near Regina. Verna didn't let on, but she recalled him working with a telephone crew building lines in that area. As disturbed as he was, he had a very good memory.

After having a sane conversation with Verna, he again became extremely disturbed on the drive to North Battleford. Although he was of small stature and weighed only about one hundred and thirty pounds, he managed to kick the rear window out of the police car. Verna was glad he had behaved himself while in her kitchen.

Detachment life for Verna was relatively short, but she looks back on the experience with fond memories.

Spiritwood, incorporated as a village in 1935, is in the heart of Saskatchewan's Lake District and situated on historic Carlton Trail. The trail is clearly visible in several places. The RCMP opened a detachment there in 1929. Agriculture, government services and tourism support the community. There is fly-in fishing at four area lakes.

46

Elise's Detachment Education

One of Elise Reed's memories about living in North Portal comes with a distinctive odour. The living quarters were adjacent to the detachment office. The door to the office was closed at all times. One day when Elise's husband, Ted, returned to the office, he opened the adjoining door briefly. He reminded her, in no uncertain terms, to keep the door closed, and to not enter the office for any reason. She was quite puzzled why that day was different from any other.

About an hour later, Elise noticed Ted left with another man. Curiosity finally got the better of her, and she cautiously opened the door, not knowing what to expect. She was immediately assaulted by revolting odours beyond belief. Elise quickly shut the door, wishing she hadn't been so inquisitive, and it took her some time to recover. She later learned her husband had picked up a transient who wore every article of clothing he owned; there were layers, and layers of filthy clothing saturated with an accumulation of body odour. Elise had never encountered a scent that disgusting, and she still remembers it with a shudder.

Elise performed the usual duties of filing and answering the office phone or radio when her husband was out. One day Ted, sounding frantic, called her over the radio. He hurriedly asked her to call the Estevan detachment to send a member *pronto*, as he had locked handcuffs on a prisoner, and during the struggle, the handcuff key had been lost. He was concerned that the cuffs were on tight enough to damage the prisoner's wrists. Elise relayed the message as she was asked, and soon help was on its way. All ended well, but illustrates difficulties encountered when members of the Force were obliged to work alone.

Leaving their southern posting, the Reeds travelled to their next detachment of Spiritwood in northern Saskatchewan. Although it is a much larger detachment point today, it was a one-man office then. This was the first time Elise had encountered native Canadians. She was amazed at the papoose "carrying basket".

Within their first week at Spiritwood, Elise had a memorable experience. It was late at night when she was awakened from her sleep by strange noises. Since Ted had gone out on patrol, she initially wondered if he had returned, but realized he wouldn't be making those noises. It sounded as if someone was stumbling around and falling into things in the living room below. She grabbed her housecoat and snuck down to the living room. She encountered an obviously intoxicated native woman who was foaming from the mouth and weaving badly. Elise was very frightened, but tried to appear firm when she asked her what she wanted.

"I want my bottle," came the reply.

"I don't have your bottle. Now get out of here," said Elise. The woman just stood looking at Elise, so again trying to sound authoritative, Elise attempted unsuccessfully to steer her toward the door. The big woman remained where she was, so Elsie tried pushing her. That proved impossible since, at 115 pounds, Elise was at a great disadvantage. She was becoming quite frightened at that point. She noticed a light across the street where she ran for help. A young man and an elderly woman came to her rescue by helping to remove the intoxicated woman.

The moment Ted arrived home, he knew there had been a problem, as the smell of liquor still permeated the air. When he heard Elise's account, he told her they should have placed the woman in the cells downstairs. Crestfallen, Elise replied that she had not been thinking clearly.

At the time of this incident she was just twenty-four years with three children from ages six months to three years. Although the Reeds remained in Spiritwood only ten months, it seemed like a lifetime to Elise.

47

Unique Quarters

Eunice and Ken Campbell were at the one-man point of Strasbourg, Saskatchewan, from 1953 to 1955. The transfer took place back when the Force provided its own moving van and driver. Eunice, who was six months pregnant, and Ken packed their belongings and helped to load and unload. They weren't overwhelmed with furniture, so the packing itself presented little problem. Eunice held her breath hoping everything would arrive intact and with no major scratches.

Upon arrival at the detachment, they found the departing family's furniture in the living room, so their own belongings were unloaded into the kitchen and onto the street. Eunice was thankful it wasn't raining.

The quarters were truly unique. The wood frame, two-storied building housed the office, which opened into the kitchen. The kitchen led to the living room and two very small bedrooms. A door from the second bedroom led outside. The front room door and office door opened directly onto the public sidewalk.

Attached to the building was the fire hall, which housed the fire truck, the large town cistern, and the police car. Perhaps the most novel situation about these quarters was a door from the living room opening directly into the fire hall. A trap door led into the basement. The children thought the fire truck a marvellous addition to their home.

Eunice was further amazed to discover that the second floor housed the Masonic hall. She was thankful that it was used only once or twice a month. Every board in the floor creaked and, together with the strange rapping, made for some interesting speculation. This extremely old building held even more peculiarities for the new residents to ponder. It was held together with steel rods, which were stabilized by large steel plates on the outside of the building. Three of these rods went through the living quarters, creating a decorating dilemma.

The entire place was heated by steam heat. The last winter of the Campbells' residency, the furnace burned eighty tons of soft coal. At least they didn't have to shovel all that coal, as a janitor looked after that department. The furnace had a tendency to blow off steam periodically. The first time Eunice heard the hissing and rumble, she phoned the janitor in a panic. She and the children thought the place was about to blow up. They were told they were lucky the furnace had released some pressure, otherwise they would have been airborne. What a racket it made, but every time they heard it thereafter, they breathed a sigh of relief.

The kitchen had an old-fashioned coal and wood stove, and although Eunice had been raised with this type of facility, it had been a long time since she had cooked on one. This contraption swallowed eight tons of hard coal every winter.

One would think that with all this coal burning merrily, the family would have, at least, been warm. Not so. All winter they had two inches of frost under the bed in the so-called master bedroom. Eunice learned to cope with that, but when her son's sheets froze to the wall in his room, she felt it was a little much. She happened to mention to the town mayor that their quarters were a bit cold.

He drew himself up and in no uncertain terms said, "I'll have you know we spent two hundred dollars on that building last year." Sure, she thought, they bought some paint, which we applied. She wanted to offer to exchange houses with him, but didn't have the nerve to say anything further.

Just off the kitchen was a tiny room, supposedly a bathroom. It was here a wooden toilet, supplied with a ten gallon pail, was housed. Whenever the "honey bucket" had to be emptied, there was a path quickly cleared to the back door. Eunice's greatest fear was the bucket would spring a leak as it was being transported through the kitchen. It was not considered a fun job.

Their tub was an old fashioned round wash tub, which they'd place in front of the kitchen stove's oven, then they'd dip water from the stove reservoir, and bathe. Eunice never found it to be a relaxing bath, unless she draped her legs over the side, making a bath somewhat pointless.

Her mother bought them a two-burner stove with an oven, which proved a godsend in the summer. With small children, doing laundry was an almost daily occurrence. Ken and Eunice would fill the tin boiler the night before with water pumped from the kitchen cistern. They'd place it on the burners, and as one of the children invariably woke up at 5:30 a.m., Eunice would get up, turn on the burners, and have the washing on the line by 7:30 a.m. The neighbours never mentioned it, but Eunice thought they often wondered what that crazy woman was doing hanging wash out at the crack of dawn. In the winter, clothes were draped on a clothes horse, put out the back door, and carried in stiff as boards. It helped to be young to endure that, especially with two children in diapers.

With the office door opening directly off the kitchen and with no sound proofing, conversations and radio messages from the office were quite audible. The police radio could only receive messages. Broadcasts from Regina came on at 10 a.m. and 4 p.m., and all items were copied in a book. If Ken was out at these times, it was Eunice's job to copy. She recalls being promised a cent an item, however she can't remember bothering to collect the paltry sum.

Answering the phone and door was also part of her routine. She sometimes thought people deliberately waited until Ken left and then the fun would begin.

A job she didn't mind doing was giving the written part of a driving test. She was accused more than once of passing someone because they were "nice".

The cell was housed in the dirt basement where all that coal dust drifted around. It wasn't inhabited too often, but when it was, Eunice was expected to feed the poor soul. She was thankful they lived in a fairly law abiding area.

The Campbells lived in these quarters for two years, when it was decided it might be wise to find more suitable housing. Ken finally found a nice place that would serve the purpose. About a week before they were to move, orders came through transferring them back to Regina.

Like other wives at one-man points Eunice was expected to be the "second man". It made for an interesting life and in retrospect she was glad of the experience.

Strasbourg is northwest of Regina and between Last Mountain Lake and a high elevation called Last Mountain. Its name is derived from Strassburg, Germany but when that city was returned to France, the spelling of the name changed to reflect that.

In 1884 the first white settlers came and traded with the Indians; fish for bread and salt pork. In 1905 the first RNWMP members obtained meals for themselves and their horses from the settlers. In 1908 the detachment located in the new town hall, and had an office, bedroom and two cells. The detachment moved into Hove's house on the Crescent in 1955.

A new detachment was built in 1967. There are currently three members stationed at the Strasbourg detachment and it is considered a Community Detachment. Southey Detachment is Strasbourg's Host Detachment. The town population is 826.

48

Krugers at Cumberland

Stella Kruger has fond memories of the time she and Hal and their two little girls lived in Cumberland House, Saskatchewan. Their stay was from August 1973 to July 1976. Anyone that has been into a small Northern Saskatchewan community knows that it usually has a plentiful supply of youngsters and a large number of dogs. The dogs are primarily used in the wintertime for travel on the trap lines and for recreational dog sledding.

Stella recalls a lot of apprehension arriving in Cumberland House in early August, 1973. She had put her young family to bed in their tent trailer the first night because their personal belongings had not yet been set up in the detachment house. She was finally getting some fitful sleep, between slapping mosquitoes and trying to get comfortable on the "mattress" in the tent trailer, when the howling started. It was around 1:30 a.m., with the moon high in the sky. The children woke up immediately, but Hal, of course, slept soundly on. She finally got him awake and he said, "Don't worry, Dear. It's only the sled dogs." They kept up their "Welcome-to-Cumberland House-Howl" until dawn. The family pet, Snoopy, a small but fiery little Boston Terrier, also slept fitfully that night between the two little girls.

The little Boston Terrier adjusted to the wild north quite nicely even though he did have that rather scary beginning. Stella first realized how protective he had become one very cold night in February during their first winter in Cumberland House. Very loud barking and cursing near the back door awakened her. Her husband, the protector, slept soundly on until she was finally able to waken him. He pulled on a robe and went to investigate what was happening. He found a very cold and determined chap, a local veteran from the Second World War, looking for a place to sleep. Just as determined was their Snoopy to ensure the man would not get into the house. Hal, who wanted to get dressed, was also trying to put the man outside. He intended to put him up in the detachment guardroom across the compound.

About thirty minutes later, Stella's protector got back into bed, after first putting the veteran to bed and hiring a guard to watch him. Not only did he awaken her with his cold feet in her back, but also with his quiet laughter. It seems that their protective, "wannabe" police dog, had bitten Hal in the ankle during the tussle to put the man outside. Wrong ankle, good effort.

This little guy was always trying to help. One afternoon when Stella looked across the compound, she saw one of the constables struggling with a couple of rather unruly "customers" that he was trying to put into that same guardroom. This time it was a beautiful summer day and these two fellows were simply not getting out of the back of the truck. Stella never saw anyone move more quickly than these two when she let Snoopy out the back door. He covered that fifty metres between the house and the guardroom in a straight line and up into the back of the suburban. The two guests didn't want any part of that black and white, snarling, snub-nosed puppy, and they took the three steps up to the guardroom in one leap.

Snoopy was always getting into trouble. There was the time when the spring run-off raised the North Saskatchewan River so high that a muskrat was washed into the ditch right in front of the detachment quarters. Snoopy was determined to get rid of this intruder only to find the muskrat was just as determined, and made a rather nasty gash under Snoopy's left bulging eye. This time the detachment members came to Stella's rescue, as her husband was at a meeting away from the community. They backed the Suburban right up to the front door and trucked their little friend to the Nursing Station. Seems that the community nurse used up some provincial health supplies to sew up that ugly gash.

Some of Stella's fondest memories are those nights when she would see Charlie Fosseneuve, the Special Constable, leaving the yard with the Suburban and Snoopy, standing in the passenger seat, paws on the front dash, checking out his domain. He was riding shotgun for Special Constable Fosseneuve, making sure that all was quiet in his town. It seemed only fitting that "Mr. Charlie", as the Kruger girls called him, would receive the early morning call one March day in 1976. Snoopy had been killed by a pack of sled dogs.

Snoopy was not very big, but he had a lot of heart. Stella always felt safer having Snoopy with her on those nights when her husband was away and the children were asleep. Snoopy lies by the Landing in Cumberland House, out where the members would launch their police boat, and where he loved to chase squirrels by the hour.

49

First Stop – Val Marie

Myrtle became a policeman's wife when she married Constable Lorne Clarkson Rooney on Christmas day, 1939. They had a quiet wedding at her parents' house in Climax, Sask. They chose that date as her parents could close their store for the day and, as well, they had married on December 25, 1912.

Myrtle and Lorne lived in Val Marie's RCMP detachment quarters. The office and jail cell were at the front of the building, and their living quarters were in the rest of the house. All the rooms, except the office, were very small. By the time they got their piano and furniture moved in, they were quite cozy, and when they had visitors it was cozier. To deal with the necessities of life, they had the facilities of coal and wood-fired stove and furnace, and the option of outdoor or carryout "biffies".

Lorne instructed Myrtle not to do any of the police work, just be a housewife. There was a phone in the office, but all the phone calls went through the telephone operator. If Lorne were going to be out of town, he would tell the operator, and she would deal with any calls that were for him. Myrtle was not bothered unnecessarily, but sometimes she was pressed into service.

It was wartime in 1940. Anyone owning a gun was supposed to take it to the RCMP detachment to have it registered. One day when Lorne was out helping the policeman at Ponteix, all the farmers and ranchers in the vicinity decided to take in their rifles and other guns. Since Myrtle couldn't register them, and the farmers didn't want to take them back home, she tagged each with its owner's name and stacked them along the walls in the office. When Lorne came home that night, he was faced with an office full of guns.

Most of the people in Val Marie were French Catholics who spoke both French and English. Rooney's next-door neighbours had a family of eleven children, aged from one to twelve. When the Rooney's first-born was two years old, he loved to play with them, and was accepted into the family as if he was the twelfth child. He even learned to say a few French words and phrases, and could count to ten in French.

A large dam had been built at Val Marie, which provided irrigation for the town and vicinity. There were garden plots available nearby, so

"Hi dear ... I'm back. Hope you weren't too bored while I was away ..."

Myrtle and Lorne grew some vegetables. Later, Myrtle learned how to can vegetables and make pickles. She even learned how to can chicken, when she and a neighbour lady built a chicken coop and raised twenty young roosters. The women chopped their heads off, plucked and cleaned them before canning. Myrtle's life style was definitely changing.

Val Marie, formerly called White Mud, is located on rolling prairie with its coulees and creeks draining into Frenchman River in southwest Saskatchewan. The last large buffalo hunt took place near Val Marie in 1885. The NWMP began policing the area about 1873, and an RCMP station was established there in 1927. Val Marie became a village in 1926. The CPR came in the late 1920's.

Homesteaders travelled to this ranching country from eastern Canada, Europe and the U.S.A. Its population is 160. The Grasslands National Park was created southeast of Val Marie. The community's economy is based on farming, ranching, tourism and natural gas. It is home to the only prairie dog town in Canada.

The Rooneys moved to the Cabri detachment in 1944. The front entrance was for the living quarters and the side door for the RCMP office. If there were prisoners in the cells, Myrtle would be obliged to make their meals. If Lorne was not in the office, she was expected to answer the phone, and to contact Lorne if she could. Sometimes she phoned the RCMP Headquarters at Swift Current and they would relay the message by car radio.

Many times, people would come to the front entrance instead of the side door to ask for the policeman. One evening, Lorne's mother was staying with Myrtle while he was out of town. Myrtle answered the front door and there stood a man and two ladies. The man had blood dripping from his head onto his face. He had not bothered to clean it up because he wanted to show the policeman what his wife had done to him. She had hit him with a beer bottle. They thought Myrtle was supposed to know what to do about it, so she had to be as diplomatic as possible.

After she quietly got rid of them, her mother-in-law said, "I sure would not like to be a policeman's wife." Myrtle laughed, and said it wasn't too bad and often very interesting.

She appreciated the large rooms in the house, but the kitchen floor was weird. It had a hump all across the middle of the floor where it had heaved up. They had to balance the kitchen stove and table over this hump. When their son turned three and had a tricycle, he would ride up the hump and coast down the other side.

The Rooneys moved to a three-man point at Watrous in 1949. They lived in a home separate from the office, so there was no more police work for Myrtle.

Cabri celebrated its 90th birthday in August of 2002. It is ranch country located in southwest Saskatchewan, its north boundary being the South Saskatchewan River. Its population is 511. Hunters come from around the world to hunt antelope, deer, geese and ducks. Cabri gets its name from a derivation of a voyageur's word for pronghorn antelope seen in the area. The voyageurs and French Métis thought the pronghorn antelope in the area looked something like a goat. Cabri is the French-Provincial name for goat.

Cst. J.D.L Gray was the first member to serve in Cabri, opening the detachment in May of 1932. The Police Barracks were rented at $25.00 per month from Mr. Carl Cornelson. October of 1936 saw the detachment move to the Gimby House on Main Street; Mr. Oswald Gill owned this building. A new building was occupied in December 1964, and this is the present-day detachment which has been renovated twice. There are three members serving the town and area. A former member of the North West Mounted Police is buried in the Cabri Cemetery.

50

The Survival of Betty Cheavins

Betty and Mel Cheavins were married in 1960, but prior to their marriage they had an unusual courtship. They became acquainted in *small town* Saskatchewan when Mel was a young constable stationed with the RCMP and Betty was a twenty-year-old telephone operator.

From the 1940's to the '60's, the local telephone operators assisted the Force by supplying information and relaying messages. A special red light was installed on a Main Street pole, and the operator on duty activated it whenever she needed to contact a policeman. There might be an accident, a break-in or other emergencies to report. When a fire call came in, the operator set off the alarm. It was the operator's duty to take details regarding any emergency before contacting the police and other appropriate people, possibly the ambulance driver or physician, giving them directions and other details. The policeman on duty made regular checks of the red light as he went about his work. If he was going out of town or was to be out of his police car for any reason, he'd alert the operator. She knew of his whereabouts at all times.

Experienced operators were put on the night shift alone and for three months consecutively. That way the public was insured information was taken with speed and accuracy.

Country bred telephone employees had an advantage over city girls who found themselves working in a small community. The latter had difficulty in sorting out directions for dispatching, and they didn't always know the right questions to ask. Betty remembers one particular call she handled that might have given a city bred operator a problem.

"There's been a bad accident – Rex rolled his tractor in the south quarter – get the police out right now." It wasn't the usual habit to ask for the ambulance; it was police, doctor, and then ambulance. The operator was sure of only one thing, the name Rex, but a last name was not given. (Perhaps it was the family dog). Where the heck is the south quarter, another operator might have thought, and what is a quarter? Attempting to maintain a controlled approach, Betty asked questions until she had more detail.

"Go out of town past the elevators, down the road to the old Graham place; turn at Yeske's straw pile, the old one, not the new one."

It was a very dark, rainy evening, and a policeman was expected to recognize the old straw pile. Betty concentrated on gaining the caller's co-operation.

"That was difficult to do," Betty said, "as farmers in the area considered telephone operators to be weaklings. They couldn't haul two pails of slop to the pigs at once, five gallon pails at that." With persistence she got answers to questions such as left or right, and the number of miles involved. By then, the farmer's wife was screaming in the background,

"Hurry, the man is dying under the tractor." Upon investigation it was discovered the man was cold dead, having rolled the tractor in the afternoon, and the farmer happened to notice him hours later, when, with much excitement, he contacted the operator. She had decided to call the doctor and the ambulance as well as the police.

There were consequences early next morning when the Sergeant-in-Charge contacted the Chief Operator to inform her that the night operator had better sharpen her information-gathering skills, since the ambulance and physician were unnecessarily dispatched. He further pointed out, the situation represented a cost in time and money to the ambulance and physician, not to speak of a possible need for their presence at another emergency. The operator hung her head for a few days. She noticed no one remarked at her ability to spend time on the farmer's call while handling the switchboard that was "lighting up like a Christmas tree".

The same operator felt better on the day she was able to help in the safe delivery of a baby by facilitating a three-way telephone hook-up. A farmer's wife who was alone when she went into premature labour, contacted the operator. A call to the RCMP office resulted in a patrolling member being dispatched to the farm. After assessing the situation, the policeman had the operator locate the local physician, and had her provide a hook-up from the farm to the physician, and also to the husband who was working several miles away. The policeman delivered the baby with coaching from the physician, while the husband encouraged his wife and received regular progress reports.

Betty recalls other successes that made her feel good about her job. From the switchboard she was able to facilitate the recovery of a child's lost pet. Betty handled one message with tongue-in-cheek; a woman phoned with concerns regarding her husband at the beer parlour. The wife was worried he might not be fit to drive home to the farm in the storm. Betty dutifully passed the message to a policeman. Because he was new in town, she explained which pub door to enter when dealing with family concerns or disputes. By then another urgent call came in. There was new information about a culprit planning to leave the Greyhound Bus at a station other than where a policeman was waiting. Betty was able to relay this important information.

Once Betty and Mel had become well acquainted through work, they began dating. Following their engagement, Betty entered another training program. After Constable Mel Cheavins popped the question in 1959, and received a favourable reply, Betty learned of the *Big Rule*. Members wishing to marry must be twenty-four, have five years' service, $2,000.00 in the bank and no debts. The *Bigger Rule* required the prospective bride and her family to undergo the *Big Investigation*. After her groom-to-be was summarily ordered into the presence of the Officer Commanding, Betty learned of a new hurdle.

"In the Officer's opinion, members should not go out with telephone operators," Betty said, "let alone marry one. He advised that he thought members would do well to look at someone like a nurse or a teacher as they had a higher standard of education."

After hearing that news, Betty had little time to recover before she discovered the *Big Investigation* was underway. Oh, boy, she thought, has the Force got a surprise coming. Betty's uncle, her Dad's brother, was serving a term in a Calgary jail for the 1942 axe killing of a native. The man had tried to steal the uncle's horse from the stable behind the beer parlour in a small town. Betty got the *Investigation* news from her valiant fiancé.

The O.C. had informed him in a commanding way, "Constable, you are not marrying this very young girl." Then twenty-one, a crushed Betty didn't think of herself as especially young. Several months later, Betty's persistent Mountie reapplied for *Permission to Marry*. A new stumbling block had surfaced. The Force had discovered that Betty's seventy-year-old grandparents had come from Romania, a Communist country. *Permission to Marry* was denied – "No, No, No!"

True love was victorious, since, upon reapplying some months later, permission was finally granted. There was a small catch; the wedding date coincided with the date Mel was to be transferred from Saskatchewan to Newfoundland. More discussion ensued between Mel and the *Powers That Be*. The move to Newfoundland was cancelled. The groom was to be put on three months of nights with three days off for the wedding, the third day to report for night duty.

Mel and Betty were transferred to a small Saskatchewan centre where French was the main language spoken. English speaking residents were not readily served at the only drug store, and the policeman was not welcome to sit with the local people in the restaurant. Betty had trouble locating a hairdresser who was not "booked up". When she succeeded in making an appointment, the hairdresser spoke over her head to other customers, and in French only. It was difficult for Betty to shop for groceries, as the clerks spoke no English.

A most trying time for her was when she made early afternoon doctor appointments. "I sat in the waiting room until 5 p.m. when all the other patients had been seen." After the birth of her first child she found the locals would not allow their children to play with her little one.

Home was located twenty-eight cement steps above the post office, while Betty's ringer washer was housed in the basement, a further twenty-eight steps down. There was a long string hanging from one light in the middle of the basement, a string that was difficult to find in the dark. Clothes drying resulted in another issue. Feeling quite inventive and independent, Betty strung up a clothesline in the cavernous basement room. It would serve quite well, she thought. Other than Betty's washer and line, this basement room held nothing but a sewer hole. Even so, the postal authority considered it "a disgrace" to hang laundry in this building. Laundry was not to be left unattended in the basement. Down came the clothesline. Pregnant Betty with small child in tow, carried laundry down, one load at a time, then back up all those stairs for drying.

Betty thought their kitchen was large enough to "house a small dairy herd." When she stood on a chair, she was able to reach only the bottom shelf. Each of the two bedrooms could barely accommodate one 48" bed with space to walk sideways to get into bed. There were huge radiators with hot water heating. The caretaker lit the furnace, which was housed in a basement room with a heavy locking device. Some heat would finally trickle into their radiators two or three hours after the furnace was lit.

Another problem was the large tub and cold water. Even a shallow bath required twenty kettles of boiling water. By the time the eighteenth kettle was hot, the first water was cooling. The tub was so large, Betty considered "a grown family of four could have taken a bath together." Because the town water was so rusty, the tub's bottom was obliterated. The kitchen sink's brown bottom remained visible when dishes were being washed.

Since there were no clothes closets in the apartment, and because Mel saw only evening and night duty, Betty decided to pack away his civilian clothing.

After three years of doing the best to accommodate herself and her family to these inconvenient quarters, Betty was anxious to move out. She was expecting her second child when the *Big Inspection* was to take place. With the last few dollars before payday, Betty prepared a nice meal for the officer who would be inspecting the office and living quarters. After the officer looked around, he announced that some wives lived in worse conditions, and that Betty and her family were in "one of the better quarters."

Betty said, "I really don't mind the inconveniences so much, but it's very difficult living through Saskatchewan winters with heat available only three hours a day, and none at all when the caretaker is off and the post office is closed. It will be especially difficult with two small children." Months passed before permission was granted for the family to move.

Being ostracized by the locals, Betty and Mel found it difficult to find an alternate home. Finally, Betty located someone who knew her father, and he agreed to rent her a place. It was small and old, having a dirt basement and was without noticeable insulation. The colonies of mice moved in during the fall, and raised their many young all winter. By spring, Betty was suffering mouse stress. Even the family cat didn't want to see another mouse.

The police phone had a message-forwarding system to their home. With her husband working around the clock, Betty took messages to give to him when he dropped by every once in a while. Having a weekend off was unheard of, so there was no relief for Mel or Betty even then. The odd Wednesday off was considered a bonus. Holidays were often cancelled due to shortage of members on that detachment.

Betty found their pay was not in line with the cost of living. To augment their income, she did cake decorating for birthdays, weddings and anniversaries. Since the local community did not support her, she relied on the surrounding communities. She also sewed for herself and the children.

When their transfer came through to Torquay, Saskatchewan, a one-man, border-crossing detachment where they would live in government quarters, Betty thought she had gone to Heaven. The movers were unloading while she walked around the "castle". She was surprised when the residence doorbell rang. There stood a woman who, with oven mitts, held a roaster from which came the most wonderful aroma.

"Just a little something for your family as you move in. Welcome to our community." As the door closed, Betty stood in shock. She had not said a word, no thank-you, no what's-your-name. Feeling numb, she removed the roaster lid and discovered a mouth-watering, farm chicken, potatoes, carrots, onions, and dressing. Betty thought that was the best looking chicken she had ever seen, so perfectly shaped and evenly browned, it would be superior to any shown in a glossy homemaker magazine.

Snapping out of her dreamy state, she ran out the door in hopes of finding the angel of succulent dinners. As she hurried, she ran into another angel from Heaven, one with a pie, a fresh, homemade pie, and warm, and with another of those killer smells. Betty felt like "a queen in a new land."

When Mel drove in from his initial tour around town, and a first visit at the cafe, he had a shock to share. He reported that while at the cafe, when he sat in a corner by himself, the waitress came over and said,

"You're the new policeman, aren't you?" She picked up his cup and walked over to a table with a dozen regular coffee drinkers and said, "Sit here and I'll introduce you around." She rattled off all the names, and listed what each person could do to help this new policeman. As he told Betty his story, he seemed to be walking on air. She showed him and children the gifts of food. Everyone stared in disbelief. Although it was only June, Betty laughingly suggested it be saved for Christmas dinner.

The year that followed was just like Christmas with much kindness and giving, and with the making of many friends that became life-long relationships. Even in this paradise there were a few adjustments to make and lessons to learn.

One of the bedrooms turned out to be the office. Court was held every second Monday in Betty's living room, which boasted hardwood floors. She was dismayed to discover people attending court didn't remove their manure-caked boots.

Betty also discovered that she often had to relay messages. Mel attended many border-crossing stakeouts or roadblocks, and, at a moment's notice, Betty was called upon to learn codes for the evening's operation. The police car's radio didn't have a broad enough range for him to speak directly to larger detachment points or subdivision headquarters. Since Betty could copy Mel, she passed on messages for him. Because she often baked and cooked when alone, many cookies were burned, and pots of soup boiled over while Betty was glued to the radio, speedily moving messages back and forth. Even when she was free to go to bed, sleep was regularly broken as the radio chattered away throughout the night.

There was a new experience awaiting Betty in the basement of this detachment. It housed a bomb shelter that was a small room made of cement blocks. The empty shelter measured five feet by six feet, having a low ceiling and a door four feet high. It would be perfect as a playhouse for two little girls. Betty set up the small table and chairs, dolls, and pink ruffles. She felt quite creative, and the children had a wonderful time in their own little house.

All was well until the next *Big Inspection*, when a military voice boomed at her, "Please, remove the items from the bomb shelter, Mrs. *Cheeevens*." Adding insult to injury, the officer always seemed to have trouble pronouncing their name. The little girls had difficulty in understanding why they could no longer use their playhouse.

A short time after moving to this community, one of the children developed a high fever. Betty remembered being introduced to "Doc" while at the welcome party they'd been given. She asked the telephone operator to ring his number, and was soon grateful the operator made a habit of listening in. When "Doc" came to the phone, Betty noticed background noise of car motors, and of steel hammering and slamming. While Betty explained her daughter's problem, she was cut off as the operator said, "Oh, madam, we don't have a doctor in our community. Doc has had that nickname since he was a kid. He owns the car body shop and garage." Both mother and daughter recovered, the little girl from her fever and Betty from her chagrin.

The Cheavins family settled in, and felt very much at home. A year passed quickly. The town fathers told the visiting officer they wouldn't want to lose this policeman nor his family. The Force had other plans, however, and soon the moving van was again at their door.

They went north to Blaine Lake, Saskatchewan, a community with strong ties to European culture. There were no nearby playmates for the Cheavins children, most neighbours being in their seventies. Betty's disappointment in this and in being torn from a happy situation, was softened because she found herself in a large, comfortable detachment building. The living quarters were roomy, and she was happy to have a clothes dryer and a clothesline. Their quarters were attached to the office, a cellblock and the single man's quarters. Betty always found the term, "single man's quarters" inappropriate. It sounded like it was an apartment, but all it consisted of was a bedroom and bathroom, right next to the office.

There was a large yard with sizeable garden space for Betty to grow her own vegetables. She planned to do so, at least in self-defence, since she was surrounded by perfect gardeners, those that could spot a weed coming through the slightest crack in the soil.

One day a grandmotherly voice came over the phone, "Do you young things need potatoes? We have lots." Betty thought that was a kind offer, so off she went to claim the gift. When she arrived at the stated address, she was surprised to see two large pails of shrivelled spuds with white sprouts trailing from them. The greeting in broken-English was, "That will be six dollars a pail, very good potatoes."

"Oh," Betty said weakly, knowing she'd been had.

She handed the money to the woman who said, "For an extra dollar you can have the pails."

You'll get these rusted-out pails back, lady, Betty thought, but all she could say was, "No thanks, I won't need them," and she stumbled out to the car thinking, next year I'll be growing my own spuds.

Besides gardening and caring for her home and family, Betty was called upon for matron duties, sometimes accompanying a female prisoner to a larger centre. She was paid for these duties, and for the meals she supplied the prisoners.

Betty found herself being a substitute mother to the single man. Because she was sympathetic toward a young man in new surroundings, she would often wash his clothes, iron and mend for him. She invited him to join the family for special meals, and even lent an ear when there was a break-up with a girl friend.

With much hilarity, Betty recalled a single man at another detachment. This man with a creamy complexion, and with never a strand of hair out of place, wiped his spoon before stirring his coffee. It was evident early on that the detachment members had a neat freak on their hands. He seemed out of place on dusty, gravel roads in the area, in the smoke-filled office, and next door to a family with four children, a cat, a dog, and a rabbit. His dust-free, private car was parked beside the detachment under a maple tree leaking sap, and filled with sparrows. On noticing the problem, the young member quickly moved the car and polished it up once more.

Betty, as well as the other policemen, noticed that if he got a little dusty during mid-shift while on patrol, he returned from several miles away to shower and change his shirt. If a dog marked the car tires, or if for any reason the car got soiled, *Clean Boy* hosed it down and polished it. Naturally, this meant he would have to take another shower himself. Everyone was getting tired of him being so fastidious, besides using up all available hot water. Betty, always on the lookout for some fun, together with the wife of another member, decided to take matters into their own hands. One morning as they were having coffee together, they heard the shower start up. Mischievously, Betty hurried to turn off the main water valve in the basement. In moments, the *Clean One*, soaped and sporting a head of shampoo, appeared wrapped in a towel at Betty's door.

"Did you know the water's off?" he wailed. Betty got up from her coffee mug to try her kitchen tap.

"So it is," she said with a straight face. "I'll phone the town office to see what's going on. Maybe they'll turn it on so you can rinse off." In a few minutes Betty called to her soapy friend, "They tell me we're using way too much water. They'll turn it on for a couple of minutes only. From now on they want us to shower in the morning and evening only."

"O.K., just tell them to hurry; I'm freezing." Betty let the water run for about two minutes before turning it off again. Before long, *Squeaky Clean* took off in a patrol car. He never knew about the howls of laughter coming from Betty and her girlfriend. The other members, oblivious to the women's plotting, never knew why their young friend suddenly lost his fetish for extra showers.

Betty remembers another incident involving the same young policeman. It began when Betty was roused from sleep at 3 a.m.

"We've got a female prisoner," Mel told her. "Want to take matron duty? I've got to go out on another call."

"Okay," Betty mumbled, scrambling out of bed. She knew Mel and the other men appreciated her going to work on short notice, besides this was one of the jobs she was paid for. Another was cooking meals for prisoners. When the men were busy they didn't like to be held up. Like a flash, Betty was dressed, had her teeth brushed and her hair combed before she tore downstairs and into the office.

After one look at the prisoner, she thought, why all that grooming? In comparison, I look like a Barbie Doll, baggie eyes and all. The inebriated prisoner was in her mid-sixties, Betty noted, ninety pounds tops, barely five feet tall. Betty removed much of the prisoner's clothing so she wouldn't attempt to hang herself with it. Her breath was rank, and she battled Betty and the young constable "like an unbroken colt fights a rope."

While trying the gentle approach, Betty sustained teeth marks on her flesh, and the woman pushed her socks into her own mouth with enough force to induce vomiting. Finally socks and dentures were removed from the offensive mouth, followed by a litany of foul language. Betty and the policeman left her in underwear and sweater, and placed her on a clean woolen blanket that Betty had earlier washed and treated with fabric softener.

Moments later, it was evident the prisoner had released her bladder and bowels. In colourful language she called out, "... and bring me a blanket that doesn't smell." A difficult hour went by before she fell asleep. Much later when she woke up, she had changed from a worm to a butterfly. "May I have a cigarette and a cup of coffee?" she asked sweetly. "Can I go home now?"

Betty became quite used to this woman after repeated incarcerations.

Clean Boy placed the same woman in the cells one night. She was angry because he hadn't waited for Betty before closing the cell doors. Since the whole detachment was extremely busy, he said, "Someone will be with you shortly." A few minutes later when Betty arrived, she was greeted with a bizarre sight. The star boarder had stripped, was hanging on the cell bars "looking like a monkey".

"Rape, rape," she repeatedly screamed. All work in the office momentarily came to a stop, and every member turned to look at *Neat Boy*.

"Well, I'm glad to see you're happy about the transfer, dear ..."

"Bad, bad, boy," they teased. The young man turned scarlet, and nausea overtook him.

One cold winter night, the family dog's barking roused Betty. Their pet was barking insistently as she did whenever she sensed trouble. When Betty, clad in pyjamas, went to the backdoor to investigate, she found a large, inebriated woman sitting on the cement steps. It seemed she had found no one in the office before going to the residence door. She wore loafers without socks, a skirt without underwear and a coat with no buttons. When sleep had overcome her, she had apparently lifted her skirt, sat on the cold cement and released her bladder. When Betty helped her to get up she noticed a piece of flesh remained on the cement. Feeling no pain, she had allowed Betty to help her through the knee-deep snow, around to the front. Once in the office, Betty radioed Mel who was thirty miles away. He soon returned and took the woman to her home on a nearby reserve.

The next time the familiar van moved the family's household goods, Betty initially thought she'd gone to Heaven once more. It was 1968 when they went to another small Saskatchewan town. Mel was to be in charge, and the attractive living quarters were in a nice building complete with rugs. When the Cheavins family arrived, they were quite shocked to discover another member and his family had moved into "Betty's" new home the day before. Two members with the same service had been transferred to the identical point at the same time. What a disappointment this presented to the displaced family.

The van drivers needed to unload and be on their way, so there was no choice but to find a house. They were in a busy logging community and there wasn't a hut to be had. Finally, a very old man agreed to rent them two, one-room shacks he had put together some years before. The expected rent was too high, but there was no choice. The van unloaded basic essentials into the old building. The place was really too small for their family, which had grown to four children. Because of this dwelling's size, and since there were no closets, much of their belongings were stored in the dirt basement and the detachment garage. Family grace at supper that night included, "Let's pretend we are at a lake cottage for a holiday of one year." To herself, Betty said, if we make it through this without killing one another, the cat, or the dog, nothing else will ever get to us. They stayed in the "cottage" for a year, at which time they were transferred within two weeks of the family who was in the detachment quarters.

While living in that community, their oldest child was thirteen, and the others were approaching their teens. They had difficulty making friends, as several of the community's youngsters were sexually active, smoked, drank and swore. Many parents were separated, and their children didn't have enough parental guidance. Beyond school, sports became this new family's only interest.

When the moving van pulled up after this disastrous year, Betty felt as if she could load the chesterfield by herself. She made sure she had meals for the movers, which was a service not expected, and she never let them out of her sight. Betty was not going to be left behind for any reason. Perhaps the movers have to load another household, she had thought, and there won't be room for all our things. She needn't have worried as, with all their household belongings, they were transported to a happy situation.

Betty was thrilled to be in large living quarters with a nice back yard located in Langenburg, Saskatchewan. There was a park and a swimming pool across the street; the school was only a block away. The office included a stenographer, several members, and there were three police cars. Betty was relieved of most detachment duties she had previously performed.

She was regularly asked out for coffee, and she was pleased to hear people use her first name. Too often, in the past, she was simply referred to as the "cop's wife". It was a joy for Betty to hear her children laugh again. It was a bonus to have a meal together without someone being unhappy. The phone regularly rang for one of the children. There'd often be a dozen pairs of runners at the door. Even the cat seemed happier, now that she was no longer on mouse duty.

Mel was quickly appropriated to aid in community projects, and Betty was needed to help with sports and school activities. She was out so often that when the *Man in the Dark Blue Suit* came to their detachment, instead of Betty scurrying about to make a nice meal for him, he often took Mel out for lunch. Betty soon lost track of the names of the officers coming for Inspection and other purposes. She did not regularly meet them since she was occupied with her new interests.

During the Cheavins' stay at this point, the Force approved of a request for a new lawn and sidewalks. Betty helped care for the lawn, watering it early every morning and posting signs. The heavens opened up and it rained for days; it was just what the new lawn needed. A veritable bog developed under the green surface. By then the sidewalk was hard and in regular use. The children and their friends, the paperboy, and everyone else observed the posted signs, everyone except one man.

One day, this man heavily plodded across the lawn, leaving giant shoe mouldings in the wet, green growth. Out of the residence Betty flew like a "gobbler after the dog". She was "motoring at the mouth" causing the man to freeze in his last step. His foot was sinking into the marsh, while he glared at the woman who was in a rage. Meanwhile, the stenographer and three members were observing all of this from the office window.

When the family was gathered at the supper table that evening, Mel said, "And how was your day, Mother?"

"Well, you should have seen the drip that walked across the lawn today," Betty replied. "I caught him just in time, and I asked if he cared to pay for a new lawn. Then I asked if he was blind or if he couldn't read."

"Yes, I know. He told me on the police radio when he was on his way back to Regina. He was the *Man in a Dark Blue Suit*."

All the youngsters together moaned aloud, "Mooooooooom, if we get transferred it'll be your fault. We like it here; we've got lots of friends." The berating went on and on. Betty thought she would never live that incident down, and everyone wondered what the consequences might be. No sudden transfer happened, and the lawn grew after some repair. Months later the Man in Blue wrote a nice report about the lovely lawn. The family heaved a collective sigh of relief.

While still living at that point, Betty recalls one memorable night. A man, holding a gun, rang the detachment doorbell and announced he had just killed a man. Betty's first flashing thought was to treat the man gently, and agree to everything he wanted. Things went smoothly and he was placed in the cells in no time.

When Mel retired from the Force, Betty was happy that they each had more time to devote to other interests. She believes their children benefited from living in different communities, as they learned to get along with all types of people. She always taught her family that it was a privilege to learn from different cultures. The Cheavins live in Yorkton where both are heavily involved with community affairs.

51

Double Duty

Myrna Jamont's outstanding memory of detachment life is about an incident that took place while stationed in Vonda. It was about five o'clock on a very cold, stormy March morning in 1971 when her husband, Ken, received a call regarding a business establishment on fire in Alvena. It was believed its owner was trapped inside the residence at the store's rear.

Shortly after Ken and another policeman left, Myrna took a call with information about the incident. She was not able to reach the members by police radio since there was no reception from Saskatoon or Vonda. She tried to relay the message through Wakaw, the neighbouring detachment.

About then the baby, youngest of their four children under seven, decided he wanted to eat. Myrna had no time to dress, so she sat in her fuzzy housecoat and slippers in a very cold office nursing her baby while transmitting and relaying messages to the members at the fire. "My greatest fear at the time was that some other problem might arise and someone would come to the door looking for a policeman. There I would have been, hair a mess and in my fuzzy housecoat, while the baby was crying, and with no policeman about." It turned out all right; the messages got relayed, the baby got fed, and no one showed up at the door.

52

Cactus and Tumbleweed

Marg and Rick Commer were transferred to Val Marie, a one-man detachment located about twenty miles from the United States border. With their daughters Stacey, seven and Michelle, two and a half, the Commer family left the city of North Battleford. They knew they would be stationed in the small centre for two years, from 1977 to 1979.

It seemed to Marg they drove forever that wintry day, but the farther south they got, the warmer the weather was. As they approached Swift Current, the scenery began to change. There was no snow and trees were sparse. They saw only cactus, sagebrush, and barren fields of brown, dried grass. At Cadillac, a small town north of Val Marie, the wind was blowing with full force, and gophers were running across the road.

Seeing only an odd tree here and there, Marg recalled the saying, "If the woodpeckers wanted lunch, they would probably have to carry a lunch pail."

At last, they arrived at their destination, and to Marg's surprise, their new home was an attractive looking 1200 square foot ranch style house, with the RCMP office attached. Huge tumbleweeds had blown into the yard and were lodged in the wrought iron railings on the steps of the house and office. The surroundings looked very barren to her with no trees, only sagebrush and brown grass. Quite a change from the home they had just left.

Everyone was anxious to see their new place, so they went inside to await the moving truck. Almost immediately, neighbour children came to meet them and to find out how many children they had.

Soon, the family was touring the village to see what it had to offer. There was an elementary and a high school, a Roman Catholic Church, a grocery store, variety store, post office, garage, community hall, cafe, hockey and curling rinks; not bad for a village of 350 people, Marg thought. In the next few days, people came to welcome them to the community that was to be their home for the next two years.

The closest hospitals were at Ponteix, fifty miles away, and Swift Current, seventy-five miles away. This was a real concern for Marg with two small girls, but fortunately no one in the family was ever seriously ill nor required stitches. One day, Marg asked her neighbour, "How did you manage living here all your life so far from hospitals?"

The neighbour just laughed and said, "Oh, that's why our kids have scars; we don't go for stitches; we just tape them up." Marg concluded one had to be tough to survive in that country.

Nuns also lived in the village, and they told Marg they said prayers every time the RCMP member went by their home on a call, hoping they would have a safe return.

Spring approached and that meant many things. This was the time when rattlesnakes started moving in the pits east of the village, and wood ticks, which Marg had never seen, became a menace to people and animals. Every night at bath time, she checked the children to see that no wood tick had lodged in their skin or hidden in their hair. She learned that if one was left on, it would burrow into the flesh, and could be removed only by touching the exposed part with a hot needle to release its hold. If left under the skin, a serious infection would occur.

Spring also meant branding time for newborn calves, as the area was mostly ranching. This was the wild and woolly west as far as Marg was concerned, even though she came from a farm. A cowboy would ride into the corral and rope a calf, dragging it out so a group of wrestlers could hold the calf while another rancher would brand, vaccinate and castrate the animal. Later, all the cows and calves were taken to the community pasture for the summer and then, all the ranchers, their families and guests would sit down to a big supper.

Marg remembers an incident that happened at one of these brandings. She and Rick had thrown a blanket on the ground to sit on while having supper, not noticing they had covered some flat cactus. When she sat down, she instantly sprang to her feet, her behind full of cactus needles, which stung like fire. She tried to pull out what she could, but the rest remained in until she got home. Everyone had a good laugh, but the next time she was very cautious where she sat.

Summer was rodeo and holiday time. The Commers usually spent some of their vacation up north, going back to bush greenery and sky blue lakes.

Fall brought round up, when the cattle were brought home for the winter. Rick played hockey and Marg curled, so winter passed quickly. There was a week one winter when they were snowed in and couldn't leave the village. By the end of the week, the grocery store was out of milk, so babies went on instant powdered milk.

New babies often seemed to arrive during a storm. One woman gave birth in the country and couldn't get to a hospital. Neighbours, along with the RCMP, plough operators, people driving 4 X 4's and others on snow machines tried to get to her home. Before anyone arrived, the infant had died. At times like that the residents really cooperated with the RCMP member.

Marg attributes her grey hair to the trying times she experienced on detachments. One evening, while she was ironing clothes, the door flew open and a hysterical woman ran in, looking for the RCMP. Luckily, Marg was at home to assist the woman as she had just found her brother-in-law dead in his home.

Another time Rick was patrolling the ranches far into the bad lands, and was out of radio range when a call came about a roll-over accident. Swift Current Detachment was unable to reach Rick and asked Marg to go out and take down a few details. Stacey was in school, but as no babysitter was available, Marg packed up Michelle, and headed out to the scene. Fortunately, there was only a minor injury, so she took down names and other details as instructed by Swift Current members. When Rick got back, he completed the investigation.

Often at night or early morning, people would arrive at the door to the house, and Marg would have to go to the office to call Rick on the radio for assistance. They had been in Val Marie for almost two years before Rick finally got a recruit. This was a great relief for Marg. One day when Rick was away on a well-earned day off, the recruit took a particular phone call. In moments, there was a knock on the door adjoining the house. The recruit, being new to the village, asked Marg if she knew whom this certain person was. Without thinking she said, "She's an old lady, and she probably died." He left and was back shortly.

"My God," he said, "she cut her throat by plugging the electric knife in and holding it to her throat. She held it there until she severed her neck almost completely and fell to the floor." Seeing how upset the constable was, Marg offered her assistance. She contacted the ambulance and the coroner, as the recruit wasn't yet familiar with local procedures. Although they agreed it would have been better had Rick been there, it was good experience for a new member.

For the most part, the Commers enjoyed their stay in Val Marie. After two years, they were transferred to Maple Creek which was a ten-man detachment.

53

Harsh Penalty Follows Marriage

June Bradley was born in 1920 to homesteaders, Alert and Christina Olsen, who farmed in the Phippen and Wilkie areas of Saskatchewan. Vivian Lester (Brad) Bradley was born in 1916 in Paramaribo, Dutch Guyana (Surinam), South America. His father was an American physician and member of the American Consulate. After his death the family immigrated to Canada; Brad was eight.

Brad joined the Royal Canadian Mounted Police in 1941, and four years later he married June in Saskatoon. They had expected their first several months of marriage to be the happiest of their lives, but the RCMP had other priorities. Brad was stationed in Lanigan, Saskatchewan when the Force learned of his marriage without permission. He was escorted to Saskatoon Detachment by train, and was confined to barracks for two weeks, after which he was brought before the RCMP court. Brad was immediately dismissed from the Force on December 31, 1944 and was fined fifty dollars. Since the young couple had no money to pay the fine, June's parents provided the required amount.

The next day, Brad joined the navy, spending one year in Halifax on shore patrol duty. Meanwhile, June lived with her parents in Banff. Thirteen months later, in February 1946, Brad reapplied and was granted acceptance into the RCMP. There was, however, a stipulation. He must serve the time he should have waited before marriage on guard duty at Parliament Hill, and on single man's pay. June and Brad shared a one-room accommodation while he served at Rideau Hall, residence of the Governor General, His Excellency Viscount Alexander of Tunis. The next year saw Brad transferred to North Battleford, still on single man's pay. The young couple moved into adequate quarters built by the government for the Canadian Air Force. Their first child, Juanita was born at that posting in 1947.

Shortly after the baby's birth, the young family was transferred to Lloydminster. They paid nine dollars rent, all utilities included, for a two-bedroom accommodation located above the Post Office on Main Street. June worked part time at a grocery store. When their son, Laurie was born in 1950, Brad was finally paid a married man's allowance. During their five years in Lloydminster, the industrious couple bought a series of small houses. They worked hard to clean and redecorate them before renting them out, and selling each one as it paid for itself.

July 1, 1952 found the Bradleys in a new, one-man detachment at Glaslyn, Saskatchewan. June thought she was in Heaven to have such a nice home with all the facilities she could possibly want. Daughter Enid was born in 1953.

After only two and a half years in Glaslyn, the Bradleys were posted to Cumberland House, Saskatchewan. It was to be a three-year posting, which included an extra fifty cents per day for northern pay.

Samuel Hearne first established Cumberland House in 1774. It is an island on Cumberland Lake, and the oldest community in Saskatchewan. It is located approximately one hundred miles north of The Pas, Manitoba and near the Saskatchewan/Manitoba border. The community was named for Prince Rupert, Duke of Cumberland, and the first governor of the Hudson Bay Company. The first school in Western Canada was founded there in 1840. Cumberland is home to Cree and to Métis, descendants of Aboriginal trappers, hunters and fur traders of the area.

When the Bradleys lived there, the population consisted of about 700 Métis and 7 white families. There was a Government Trading Store, Hudson Bay Store, Department of Natural Resources Officer, a farm instructor, an Anglican Church, a Roman Catholic Church, and a convent of nuns who taught at the two schools. There was also a registered nurse at a small nursing station to look after the island's medical needs. Until a bridge was built in 1996, the only way to reach the community was by boat, open barge, plane, dog team, or bombardier. There is a present population of 1200, with 800 on the reserve. There are now five RCMP members serving the area.

In late August 1955, the Bradleys drove their family car as far as The Pas, Manitoba where it was loaded on a large, open barge with all their furniture and family belongings. For five days the barge travelled along rivers and lakes until it reached Cumberland House. June was surprised she and her family weren't expected to travel with their belongings by barge. She concluded her advanced pregnancy must have been taken into consideration, as the whole family was flown to Cumberland House. The RCMP craft fitted with pontoons, landed on Cumberland Lake.

When they saw their accommodation, they were dismayed to find it was a very old, rundown two-storied house with attached cell room. There was an icehouse for preserving food. The partially furnished house would be their home until the new quarters were completed. For their first three nights on the island, they had only one bed and no blankets or towels. An old sofa and a couple of old chairs pushed together served as makeshift beds. The following day, Special Constable Charlie Fosseneuve acquired blankets from the old cell room, sheets and towels from the Nurse's Station. Their belongings arrived in a few days, and June set up a temporary household.

They soon learned there were no telephones on the island, and the only radio was located at the Department of Natural Resources office. This was their lifeline when an emergency plane or supplies were required. There was a six week spring break-up and a freeze-up period each fall when no one could fly to or from the island. Since the new baby was due in December, it was decided June must leave early. At the end of October the D.N.R. radio received a message saying the Force plane would transport her to Saskatoon. Luckily, she and two and a half year old Enid were able to stay with June's sister Reta and her husband, Kenn, Dog Man for the RCMP in Saskatoon. Her new son, Darryl, arrived a few weeks early on November 12, 1955.

Meanwhile, Brad managed to cook meals on the wood stove, and he sent the two older children to school, fed, clean and properly clothed. It was not an easy task since there was no running water, nor refrigeration; neither was there television to entertain the children after school.

During June's absence, the new building was completed. With Charlie Fosseneuve's help, the family's belongings were moved in.

June's return to Cumberland was delayed as Darryl, at two days, contracted a staphylococcal infection that was rampant at Saskatoon City Hospital in 1955. It was mid-December when the aircraft, equipped with snow skis, flew June and her two youngest back to Cumberland. It was a happy time with the family being reunited, and June was delighted to see their new home.

There were two bedrooms and a bathroom upstairs. The living room and kitchen, complete with the old stove, but also with an electric refrigerator, were on the main floor. As usual, the office was attached to the living room, and there was another room and bathroom intended for a future second man. Alas, there were problems with this new accommodation. With only two bedrooms for a family of six, they decided to use the extra room as the master bedroom. There was a propane heater in the living room and one in the extra room, but all the floors were like ice.

The Bradleys had no experience with the new sewage system, and it did not always function properly. A *honey wagon* emptied the cesspool, and at such times, Brad and Charlie had to crawl down into it. One day, the men came up with strong smelling sewage icicles on their fur caps. Another time, June discovered raw sewage filling up the bathtub in the single man's quarters. Because there were no plumbers on the island, she learned to keep a close watch on the sewage level, and alerted the men when she thought the cesspool needed emptying.

When the Inspector arrived from Prince Albert Subdivision, he was amazed to discover there were only two bedrooms for a family of six. He was ready to arrange a transfer as soon as possible. June and Brad discussed the situation for fifteen minutes, when they agreed to complete two years at Cumberland, instead of the planned three. Their two older children were well settled in school that was run efficiently by nuns from the convent.

August 16, 1957, two years after arriving on the island, the Bradleys left for Prince Albert. They remained there until Brad passed away during the summer of 1964. June was left with four children ranging in age from nine to seventeen. She was paid a monthly allowance of $64.00 for herself and $35.00 for each child. Allowances for the boys were cut off at age sixteen and at age twenty-one for the girls. To her credit, June managed to raise her children, each of whom has done well in life. June worked in real estate for many years until her retirement. She continues to enjoy life in Saskatoon.

54

Eston Memories

When on a one-man detachment at Eston, Bunny Fox remembers how her husband, Art, went many nights without sleep. She can recall times when he would go three days without getting out of his clothes. He would sit in a chair and doze a bit, have some coffee and go again. Bunny spent many evenings sitting with him, and reading at the RCMP office behind the fire hall. They enjoyed each other's company on nights that otherwise would have been quite lonely. At times Bunny would wheel their baby's carriage into the cell as it was dark and their small son would sleep nicely there.

After a new post office was built, the detachment office and living quarters were above it. Bunny became mother to all the young recruits sent out for her husband to train. Their feet seemed to be under the Fox table quite often at mealtime, especially when it was getting near payday.

Bunny said, "I don't think the young men ever realized we might be a bit short then as well."

55

Housing Problems and Other Annoyances

It was in 1959 when Gwen and Art Reinhardt were married and stationed in Carnduff, Saskatchewan. There were no houses or apartments available for rent at that time. The best housing they could find consisted of two rooms upstairs in a house owned and occupied by a retired farm couple. The Reinhardt kitchen and living area were in one room and their bedroom in the other. They shared the only bathroom, which was downstairs, with the couple who owned the house. They lived there for several months until a small house became available for rent. They would not be impressed with that little house now, but then it was like having a mansion to live in after those two rooms.

Probably their most frustrating transfer was in the summer of 1964 when they were transferred from Regina to Radisson. The moving van that arrived to move their furniture was not large enough, so all their possessions were put into storage in Regina until a larger van was available. They were told it would arrive the next day. Being young and trusting they believed the movers.

Their baby, Brenda was six weeks old and Lori, their other daughter was almost three. On June 30th they left for their new home in government quarters in Radisson. When they arrived, they found the only hotel had a single bathroom and it was down the hall. The only refrigerator for the baby's formula was in the hotel's kitchen refrigerator.

Gwen had taken enough clothing to last a couple of days. The Reinhardts borrowed a card table and three chairs from the Lutheran church pastor and his wife. They had snacks or lunches in their new home. Luckily, there was a stove in the quarters, so Gwen could make up the formula. She then took it down to the hotel for refrigeration. Next, she bought detergent and clothes pins, so she could hand wash clothes for the children. She hung the wash on the detachment clothesline. The family spent five days in the hotel before the van finally arrived from Regina. Gwen could have kissed the movers when they pulled up to the detachment.

Upon arrival in Radisson, Art found that his second man had been taken to relieve at other detachments for holiday time. The same thing happened every summer of the six years the Reinharts were stationed there. Gwen was on her own as far as getting settled was concerned. Art had his work cut out for him; he was on his own also. The guys didn't have regular days off or forty-hour weeks in those days.

What could be called "police duties" were often part of Gwen's evenings, nights, and sometimes her days. With Art, and the second man when he was there, busy out of the office, it was expected that Gwen would be responsible for the two-way radio and the phone. She spent a lot of time on the radio and phone during their years in Radisson. The men contacted her by radio from the car or she contacted them, or was called by policemen from other detachments. Gwen often had to contact coroners and ambulances, and send relayed messages. The fellows in North Battleford referred to her as the second or third man in Radisson.

There were a lot of accidents in that area, especially at the Borden Bridge. There were also a lot of roadblocks set up in those days, as well as night patrols. The only phone the Reinhardts had in the house was an extension of the office phone. That was still in the days of the crank phone with an operator in the local telephone office.

Gwen remembers after bad accidents how the press would plague them with phone calls as they were trying to get the scoop. Sometimes, the men had been up all night, and were trying to catch a couple of hour's sleep, and Gwen would take all these calls and not give any information. She would stall the reporters as long as possible. The phone rang constantly.

There were times when Gwen checked tickets given for vehicle infractions such as faulty brakes, mufflers or lights. She would check the work orders produced by the person involved, and take their word for it that they had had the repairs done. That didn't happen often, but sometimes it involved people who had driven quite a distance for this purpose.

Art and Gwen became involved in the community, especially with curling, and they made some good friends. She's not sure she would want to repeat those years, but is glad they experienced them. When they were transferred to Gravelbourg, where there were more men, Gwen was no longer needed to help in the office.

56

Moments in Small Places

Peggy and Tim Martin moved to La Loche in the summer of 1969. Their little girls were two years and three months old, respectively. La Loche was a busy two-man detachment then, and the Martin family was the first to occupy the detached bungalow provided as quarters.

"Visiting senior members enjoyed referring to me as the *pioneer wife at La Loche*, making me sound and feel like *Mrs. Mike* or those wives who used to write things in *The Quarterly* about folding rubber bathtubs," Peggy said.

When they finally arrived after a ten-hour drive through muskeg and pine trees, the RCMP compound made them think of a nineteenth-century colonial out-post somewhere. Even without the chain-link fence that later enclosed the entire operation, the new office building and separate house, the cell block, also a separate building, the police van, the flag pole, and the huge empty space surrounding it all seemed to attest to the separateness of the "two solitudes" who lived and worked together in that community. All around were shacks, garbage, dogs fighting over garbage, and people carrying water back from the lake.

Later, Peggy began to understand why people who had lived in the community all their lives didn't want to leave. She loved the lake in the summer and occasional rides in the detachment boat along the shore on warm, calm evenings. She loved the long hours of daylight and the warm sunshine at five in the morning.

Peggy remembers trying to push the baby carriage through sand, and, one day, sitting on their front steps in tears and desperately worried. Tim had just left for Île-à-la-Crosse in the police van with several prisoners and her three-year-old daughter, very ill with asthmatic bronchitis and pneumonia.

Winter memories are darker. Peggy thinks of short grey days with seemingly endless snow, black pines, and one particularly poignant moment. She happened to glance out the window on one of those days as a small, sad cortege went by. Father Mathieu, the Mission priest, was on a snowmobile with his black robes blowing in the wind, followed by a man on another snowmobile holding a small, plain pine coffin, and finally a few more people on a few more machines, travelling from the church to the cemetery.

Another winter memory also involves children. The RCMP members sometimes were required to assist the Social Services people in removing children from family situations deemed unsafe. These cases were always sad, but Peggy remembers one especially. A young woman suffering from postpartum depression, had attempted suicide several times, and Social Services had acquired temporary custody of her baby. Tim had to go to the airport to oversee the transfer and assist with it if necessary. The mother, grieving, ill, and enraged, threatened that she would "get" his kids.

Very late one night some time later, she went to the Martin's back door, drunk and screaming. Tim and the constable were in Buffalo Narrows. There was no telephone. The radio was in the other building. However much Peggy sympathized with the other woman's situation, she was afraid to open the door. She locked the girls' bedroom door, hid the key, found something she could use as a "weapon" if necessary, and waited in the hall. Eventually the woman went away.

Nicer things happened too. At noon on New Year's Day, wearing a bathrobe, snowmobile boots, and a parka and probably hair curlers, Peggy was emptying the garbage out in the middle of the yard. Half a dozen dogs were standing around, snarling. (They always did that. Peggy had learned by then they weren't interested in her.) The church bells started ringing. They kept on ringing, and people, many, many people, came up the street, into the yard and over to the garbage bin, and began shaking her hand and wishing her a Happy New Year.

Besides the practically feral dogs, La Loche also had a number of communal horses and cows that roamed around and grazed wherever they wanted. It was not unusual to look out the bedroom window and find a horse looking back or, more typically, nibbling the new green lawn patch — sunk up to its ankles in the new green lawn patch.

Those creatures would move to a more desirable location only if someone would grab their tails, hold onto them, and run. Peggy was not comfortable around large animals at the best of times, and was especially not eager to run around and around the yard, holding a horse's tail and yelling. The children in the neighbourhood happily performed the duty whenever asked, but there never was much of a lawn until the fence went up. And many years and many lawns later, Peggy is not sure it mattered.

Lac La Loche is a Dene community. The famous twelve mile long Methy portage from Lac la Loche connected the Churchill and Athabasca river systems during the trade. Permanent settlement started in the 1930's. A school was established in 1940 and the RCMP formed a detachment there in 1967.

Early in July 1971, the Martins moved to Kyle, a four-man detachment (a four-*person* detachment, but everybody said "man" then), with the standard two-story attached quarters.

"We looked out on open prairie and I loved that. And I loved the surrounding country with its river hills and its wild geese in the fall, and the warm, hazy, dusty fall days, and the river, and even the wind that would rip a flag to shreds about twice a year," Peggy said. In fact, Peggy said she loved pretty much everything about the place, and cried all the way to the next one when they were transferred six years later.

Mostly, she remembers good friends, a wonderful little lake three miles from town where everyone had a cottage and where the Martins often went to swim and to visit. Peggy also remembers their children getting bigger and starting school, camping trips with family and friends, endless hours drinking coffee, serving hamburgers at the rink, fighting with other mothers about figure skating costumes, being on the School Board, community dances.

In small detachments, as the "wife" in the "house", Peggy sometimes answered the office phone and sometimes passed along messages on the radio when asked to, but mostly minded her own business. A couple of times she didn't mind her own business, with embarrassing results.

Most mornings in the winter, the Martin girls got a ride to school with a neighbour, a teacher. One morning the neighbour called to say their car wouldn't start. Would the Martin's? It wouldn't start either, but the police car would. Peggy was *never, ever* to touch the police car. But Tim had worked nights and was sleeping. Who would know? So, wearing the same bathrobe and snowmobile boots as in the New Year's Eve episode at La Loche, but this time with an RCMP issue parka and fur hat (with the ear flaps down), she drove everybody to school. When she got back, somebody from Subdivision was getting out of his car. Neither of them mentioned the incident to Tim.

Peggy used to laugh sometimes about the Force's surveillance activities. Then Tim told her that they had secret files on a whole lot of Kyle people, and that they kept these files in a floor safe in his office. She didn't think the constable who found her under the desk with a nail file believed her story about having dropped some paper clips.

Peggy recalls walking downtown one winter Sunday afternoon with the girls to watch the last period of one of Tim's hockey games. (She

"... Don't ask ..."

didn't like hockey well enough to watch all three periods). Several young people were standing around outside the rink and somebody said, "Here come the three little pigs." Whenever she tells this story now, people are horrified, but it really wasn't negative. That was the seventies. The police were "the pigs", but in Kyle, the "pigs" were okay, and so were Peggy and the children.

Peggy, Tim, and their family moved to Punnichy in the summer of 1977. This was a bigger detachment with more guys, (everyone still said guys), more work for Tim, and while the house was still attached to the office, less direct involvement for Peggy. She found the move hard after having put down roots, so to speak, in Kyle, but again, there were some good friends and some good times. There were many things to enjoy (along with more fights about figure skating costumes,

Brownie projects, and whether the Detachment Christmas party should take place in the house or in the garage.)

Peggy loved the yard. It backed onto a huge open space with trees and shrubs, grass and a high, steep hill that she enjoyed climbing to look out towards places she'd rather be. Things grew in Punnichy. She became interested in gardening for the only time in her life and grew pansies and pumpkins, and built a fire pit to sit around on damp summer evenings.

More than anything, Peggy tried to make living in Punnichy as "undifficult" as possible for their daughters. Many of Peggy's friends and Tim's, now are academic people who talk of having taken their children to Shakespearean plays at Stratford while on sabbaticals at Cambridge, or to Italy in the summer to look at Renaissance art. In their Punnichy days, the Martin children went off with everybody else to something called "Wilderness Camp", wearing black garbage bags with holes cut out for their heads and arms.

"In retrospect, though, I don't think living in these towns hurt any of us," Peggy said. "Our girls learned how to fit in, how to get along in almost any situation without being afraid to be a little different from everyone else. Tim and I have made some lasting friends. We have some wonderful memories (although, I have to admit, we sometimes ask ourselves why we couldn't have moved to the city sooner), and our small detachment experiences have helped us in our later careers and activities. Tim has found managing larger detachments, and later as a Section NCO of several detachments at a time, easier, I think, because of his earlier experience in these places, and as a university instructor, I know who Saskatchewan students are and where they come from."

Punnichy is a Cree word meaning "fledgling". It was thought an early trader had a similar appearance to a fledgling chicken. When it was time to name the new community, the citizens decided Punnichy suited their situation. The village is located in gently rolling Touchwood Hills and is about eighty miles north of Regina. There are four Indian reserves in the area and an RCMP detachment with eight members. Except for two years, there has been a detachment in Punnichy since 1909. In 1922 it is recorded the corporal in charge boarded at the Punnichy Hotel for 45 cents a meal. His horse was kept at the Palace Livery Barn at 30 cents a feed, including stabling. The village has grown to a population of 500.

GLOSSARY

pass muster	come up to the required standards
fatigues	clothing worn for fatigue duty
fatigue duty	cleaning up the camp
copy	message received
ten-four	I concur
e.t.a.	expected time of arrival
NWMP	North West Mounted Police
N.C.O.	Non-commissioned Officer
O.C.	Officer Commanding
C.O.	Commanding Officer
Cpl.	Corporal
Sgt.	Sergeant
S/Sgt.	Staff Sergeant
Man in a Dark Blue Suit	a Commissioned Officer

Cree words – according to Saskatchewan Indian Cultural Centre:

simakanis	policeman, soldier
chemoginusuk	soldiers
miskotakay	redcoats
astam	come, come here
iskwew	woman
moonias isquayo	white woman

SOURCES

Author's journals

Letters from twenty retired detachment wives

Letter from one wife saying "memories were too depressing to write anything."

Inspector Rebeyka, West District Officer for Saskatoon RCMP Subdivision

Sgt. Ken Burns, RCMP Planning and Archives Branch, Regina, Saskatchewan

Land of Red & White – Frog Lake Community Club, Heinsburg, Alberta

Blood Red The Sun – Wm. Bleasdell Cameron

Two Months In The Camp Of Big Bear – Theresa Delaney and Theresa Gowanlock

Saskatchewan Indian Cultural Centre, Saskatoon

Wilkie History Society

Information regarding Saskatchewan communities derived from Town Administrators, Web Sites, Saskatoon Local History Room Records.

NAME/SUBJECT INDEX

About the Author

R uth Lee-Knight has been widely published throughout Canada in such publications as PREMIUM SWIFT REVIEW, Southwest Writers Project, THE SILVER QUILLS ANTHOLOGY, Saskatoon Silver Quills Writing Club, FRIENDS AND FENCES, Prairie Lily Books, DRIFTWOOD, Saskatoon Writers Club, REFLECTIONS FROM THE HEART, The Compassionate Friends, SUBTLE VOICES, The Penhandlers, NEW MORNINGSIDE PAPERS, McClelland & Stewart Inc. and in numerous magazines and periodicals. Ruth's work has appeared in FOLKLORE, Saskatchewan History & Folklore Society Inc. and in THE QUARTERLY, RCMP Veterans' Association.

Ruth and her husband Jack, a retired member of the RCMP, divide their time between their home in Saskatoon and their lake home in the Meadow Lake Provincial Park. Ruth devotes her time to writing, practicing T'ai Chi Chih, volunteerism, enjoying her friends, family and grandchildren.